Untold Arkansas: An Anthology

Edited by Erin Wood

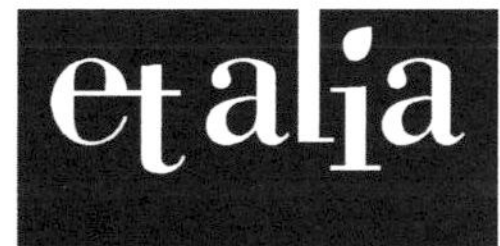

Edited by Erin Wood
Cover & Layout Design by Amy Ashford, ashford-design-studio.com

ISBN: 978-1-944528-96-6
Library of Congress Control Number: 2018912385

Printed in the United States of America

Et Alia Press titles are available at special discounts when purchased in quantity directly from the Press.
For details, contact etaliapressbooks@gmail.com or the address below.
Published in the United States of America by:
Et Alia Press
PO Box 7948
Little Rock, AR 72217
etaliapressbooks@gmail.com
etaliapress.com

Two of Wendy Taylor Carlisle's poems were first published elsewhere:
"Rumor" was first published in *Chap Book* (Platypus Press, 2016).
"Blossom" was first published in *Rat's Ass Review*, Fall/Winter 2016.

Table of Contents

INTRODUCTION

What does it mean to be from a place or to reside there? To what degree are we of or not of a place? How much of it belongs to us and us to it? Can we at once resist and embrace where we live?

As a native Arkansan who lived "away" for many years and returned more than a decade ago, I often ask myself how all my conflicting feelings for my home state can co-exist. What does it mean about me that I can love a place that can be as ruthless, heartless, discriminatory, murderous, and ugly as it can be charming, welcoming, tolerant, safe, and beautiful? For women, it serves up challenges enough; for people of color, infinitely more. It isn't unusual to find myself appalled and amazed in the same day, sometimes in the same breath. I do appreciate that with partners, family, and friends, love is a complicated thing. Might it be that place is no different?

If we did more listening to (his)stories that perhaps aren't as often heard or heeded, what might we come to understand? Who gets listened to and, of equal or greater importance, who gets ignored? Why? And what do the answers to these questions mean for us all whether we are the heard or the unheard?

In an offer to those desiring to engage with these and related questions, Et Alia Press issued a call for submissions to the Neglected Histories of Arkansas Contest with a deadline in January 2018. This collection is born of that contest, which welcomed "writings of any genre as well as visual art and photography that explore and share tough truths in and about Arkansas. . . . [to] expand cultural memory in its diversity, and shine a light on the neglected and alternative histories of The Natural State."

Tremendous thanks extend to all who submitted their work. Todd Herman, former executive director of the Arkansas Arts Center, now president and CEO of The Mint Museum in Charlotte, North Carolina, was the art and photography judge. He selected Brandon Markin as winner, and Meikel Church and Matt White as runners-up. Poet, author, and assistant professor of creative writing at the University of Arkansas at Little Rock, H.K. Hummel, was the manuscript judge. She chose Megan Blankenship as winner, and Wendy Carlisle and Bethany May as runners-up. Extensive thanks go to these judges for their time and expertise, which they gave freely in service to the project. With more voices come greater illumination, so many other submissions have also been included in the collection as well as an invited poem by Justin Booth.

This book does not pretend to be a comprehensive catalog of what plagues and elevates our state, nor is it an antidote. It is simply an attempt to encourage—with what work was submitted—vital discussions that sometimes go unspoken, to share narratives revealing treasures that can go unseen, and to offer encouragement to keep our ears, eyes, hearts, and dialogues open.

—Erin Wood

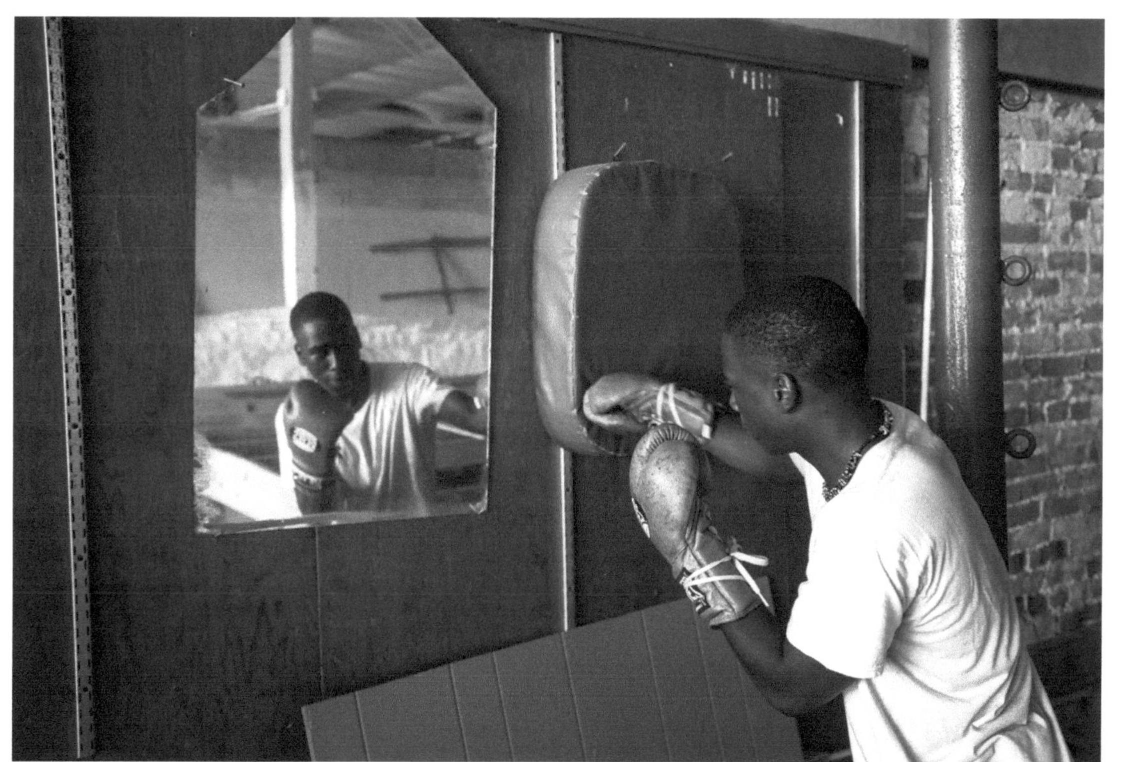

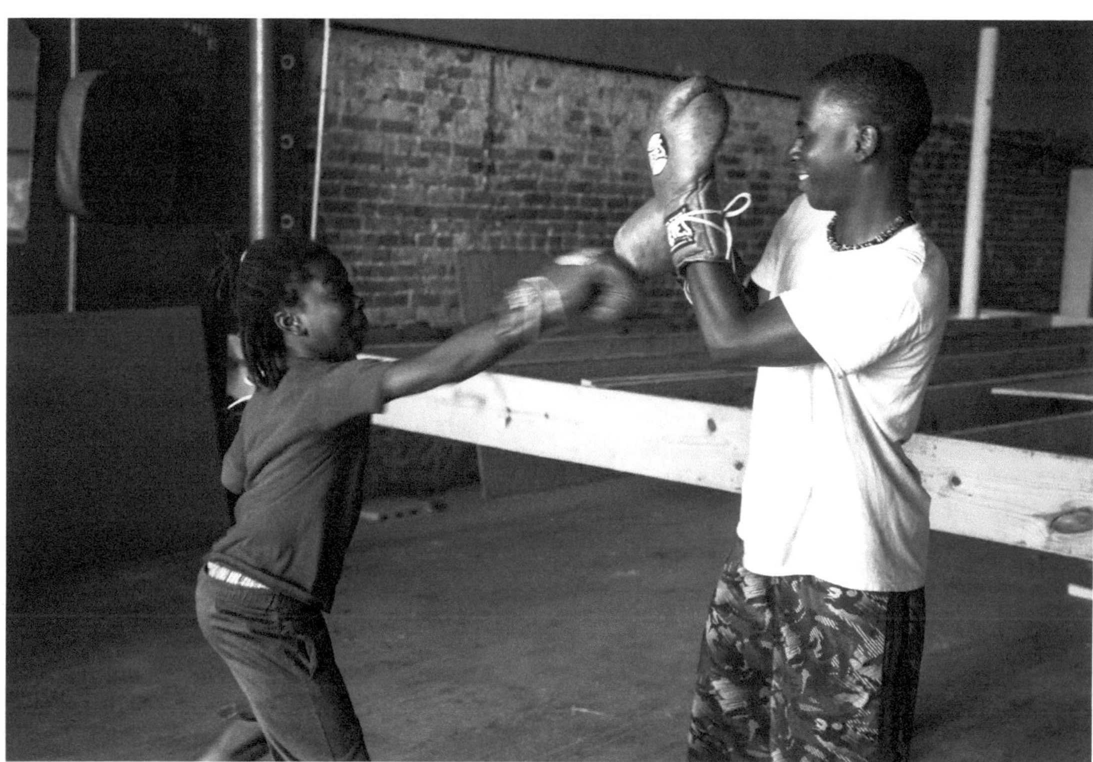

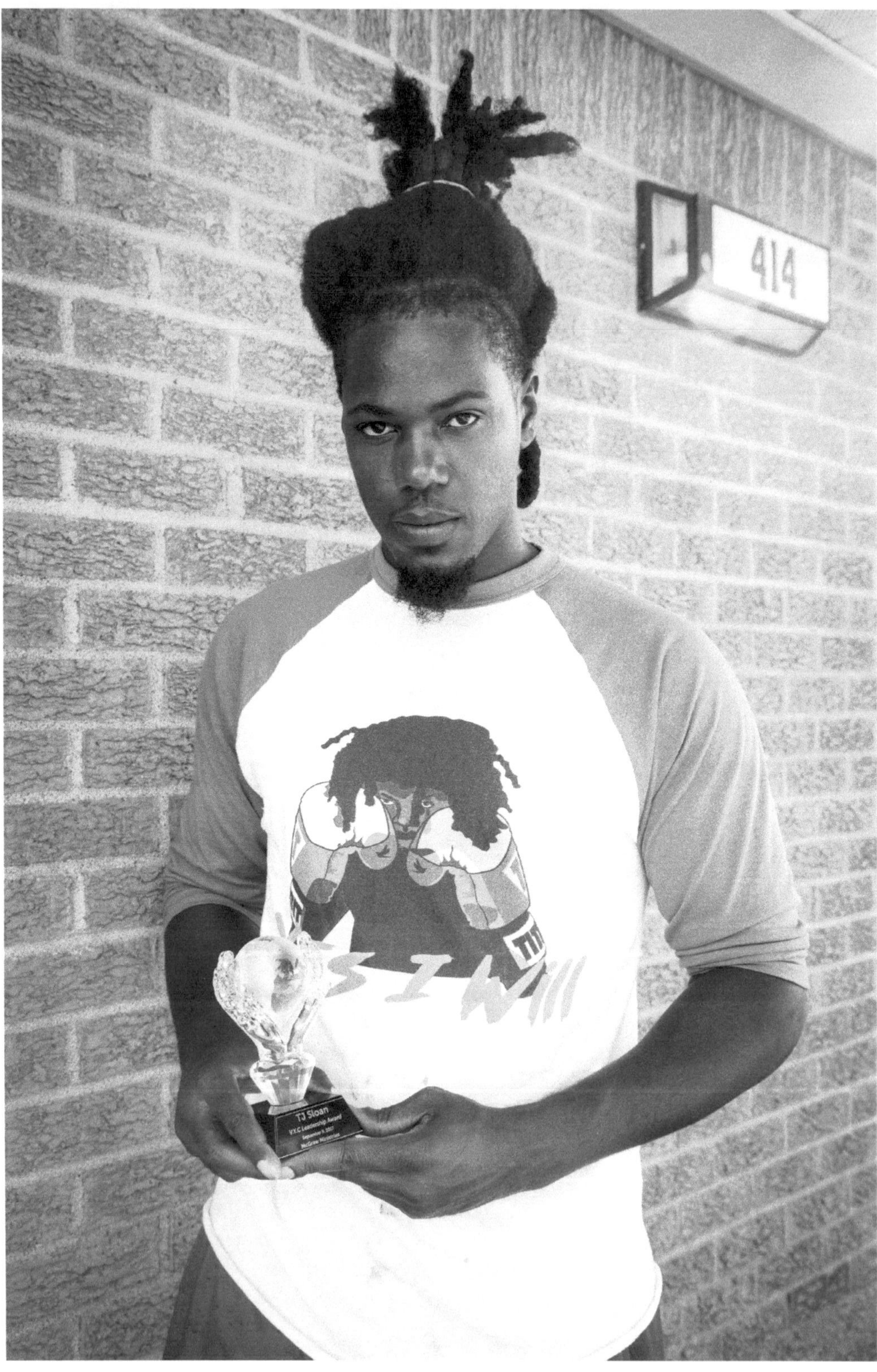
414
TJ Sloan
V.Y.C Leadership Award
McGraw Ministries

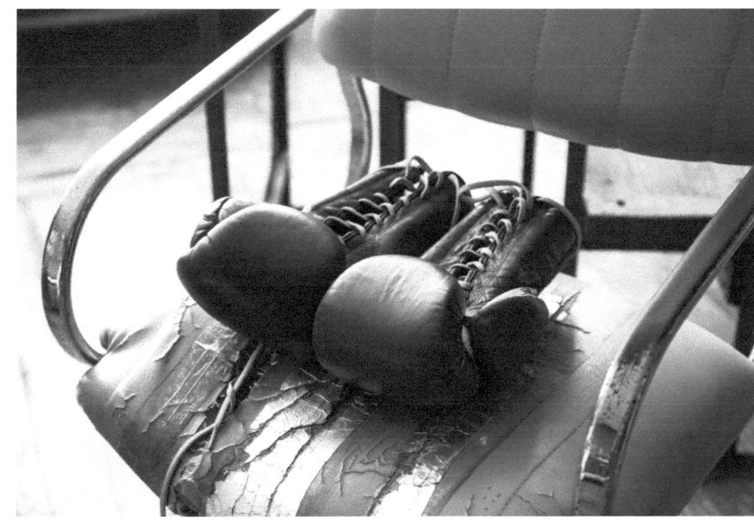

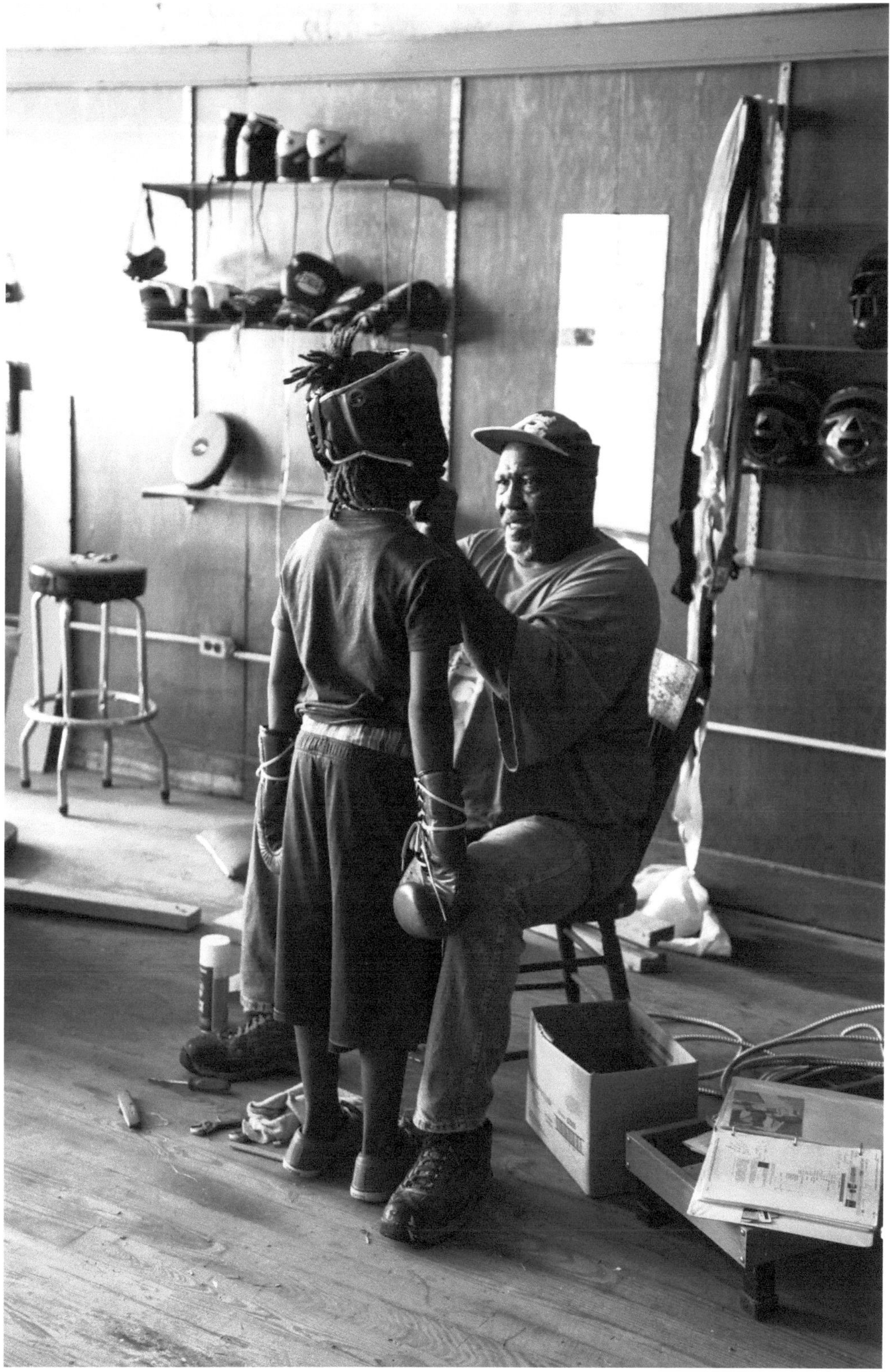

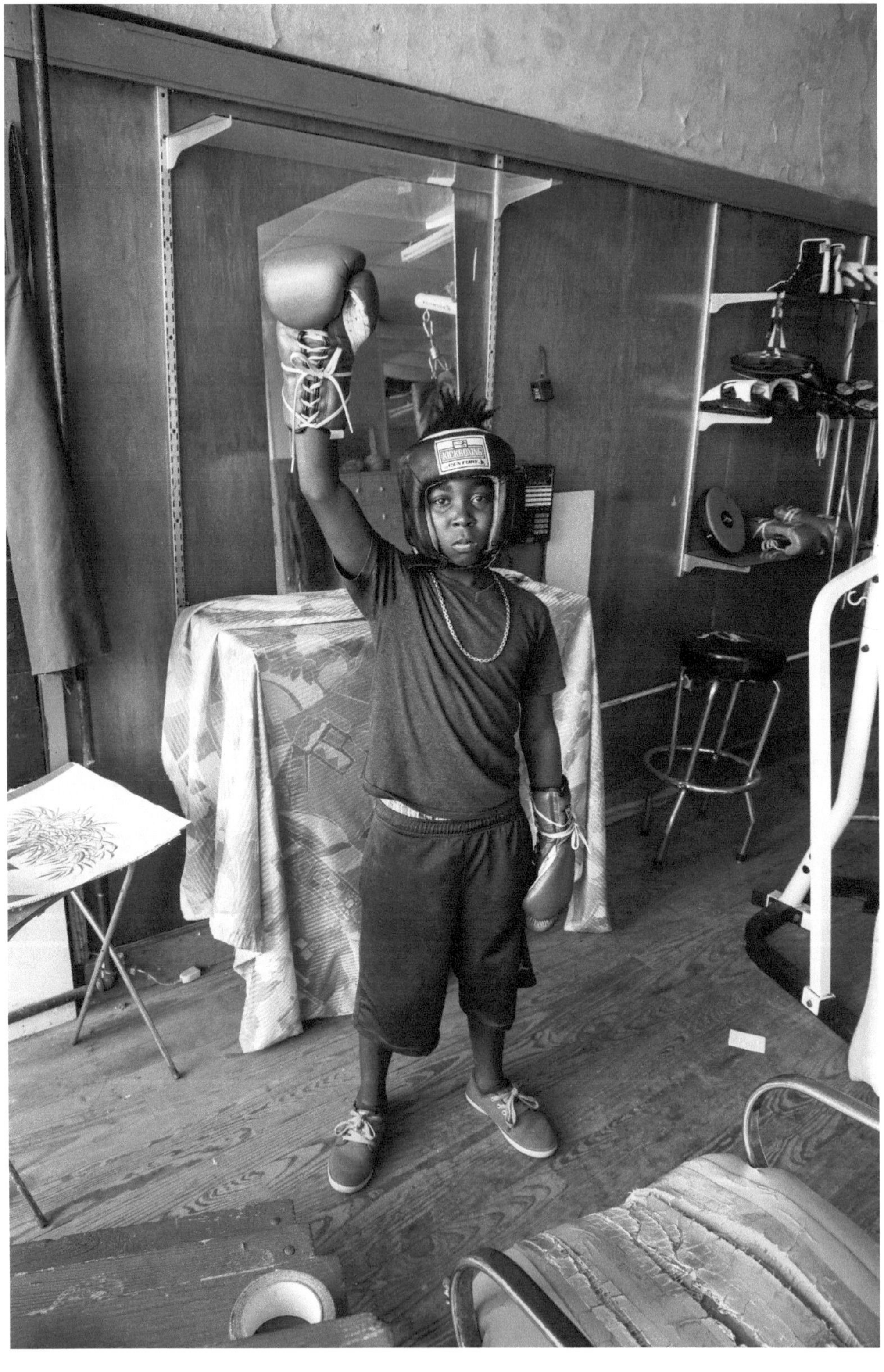

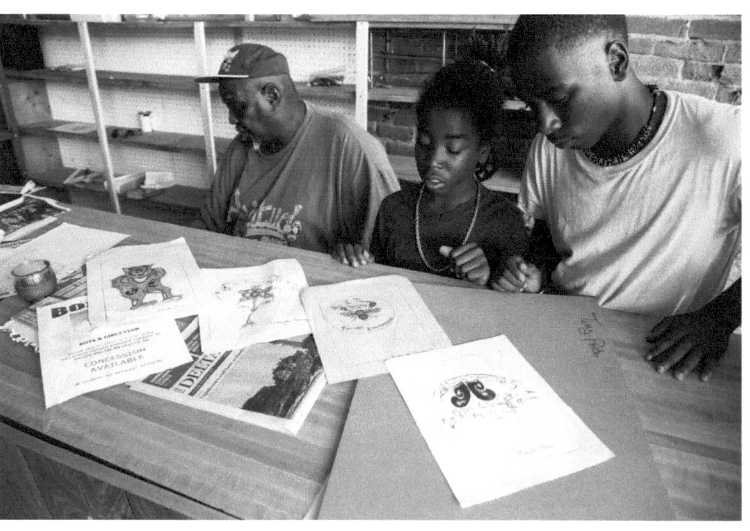
CONCESSION
AVAILABLE

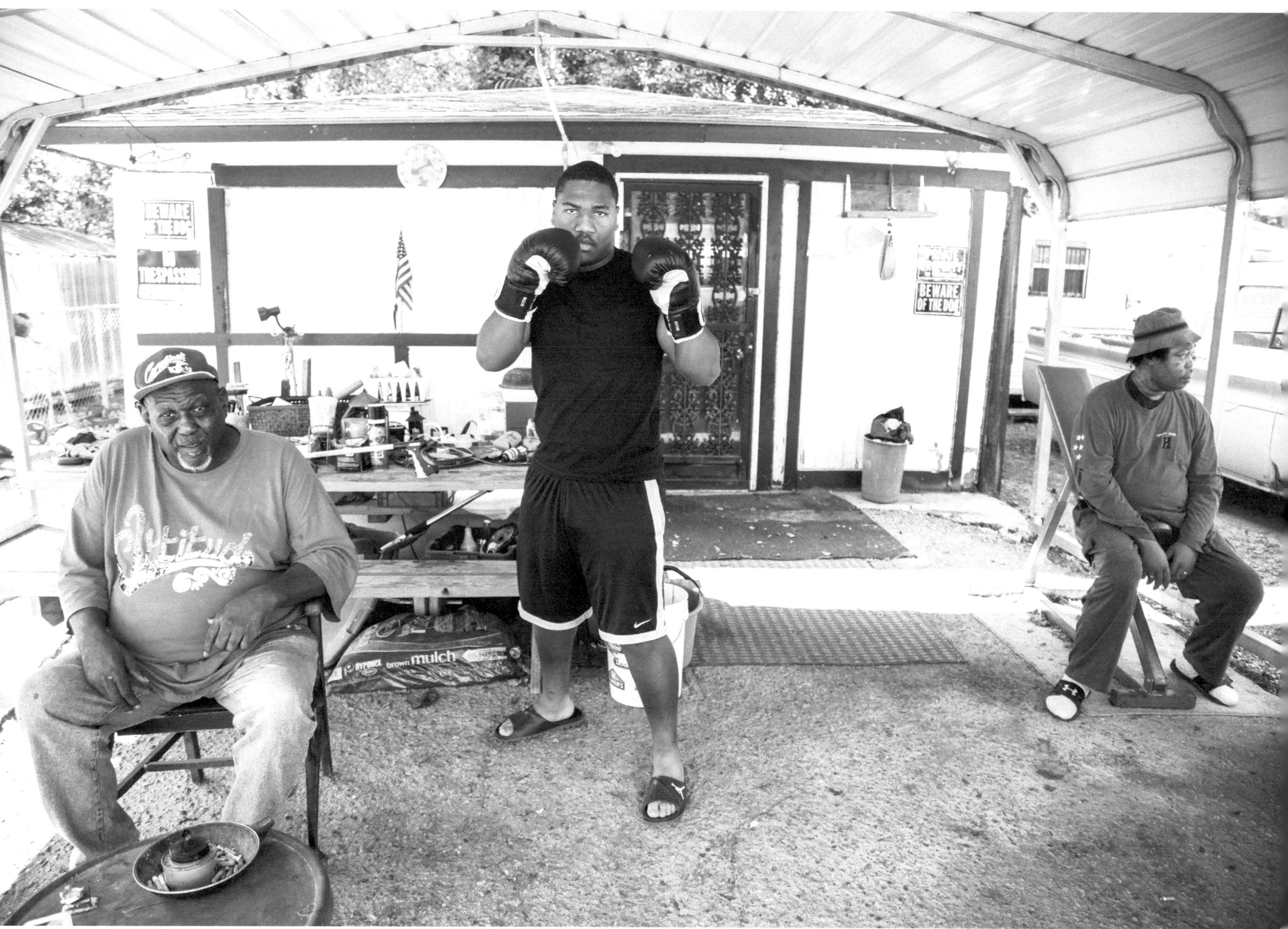
BEWARE OF THE DOG
NO TRESPASSING
BEWARE OF THE DOG
HYPONEX brown mulch

BRANDON MARKIN
Helena Boxing Club

These images document a loose affiliation of boxers in Helena, Arkansas. Despite the challenges presented by poverty and lack of opportunity, they have chosen to actively pursue a sport that requires discipline as well as mental and physical fortitude. Their story is that of many, primarily African American residents of the Mississippi Delta region of Arkansas, who work with little recognition from the world at large to improve their lives and to be positive influences on younger generations. Often the narrative surrounding the Delta is one of negativity, but to those who seek it out, there is a visible, prominent vein of positivity and hope.

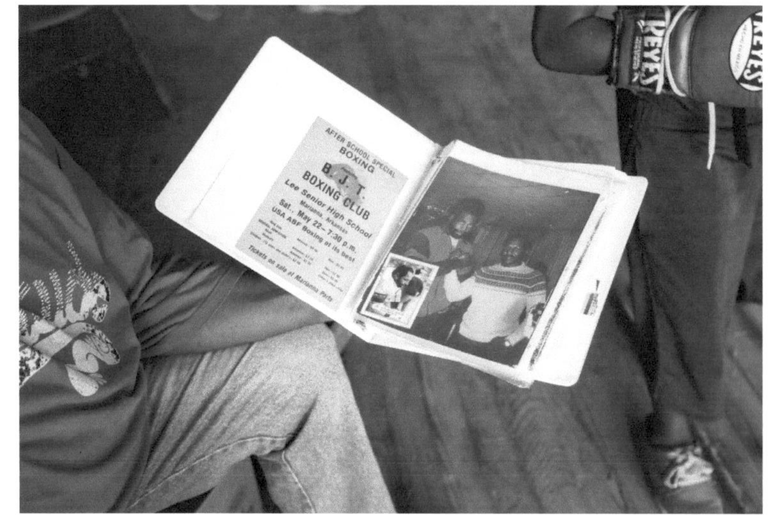

In photographing this project, I met former Heavyweight Champion of Arkansas, B.J. Thomas, who maintains a gym on Cherry Street and mentors local youths, such as those depicted in the photo essay, Jahiem Hardison and Travon Higgins. While B.J. suffers from diabetes and injuries resulting from a car accident, he still finds the stamina to put on boxing matches—utilizing the help of friends, family, and the community at large. The Helena Boxing Club illuminates a fascinating cultural history with roots in the past but with rich elements still being written.

MEGAN BLANKENSHIP
Mount Olive

Firstborn

"You ought to name her Windy. We got damn near
blowed over on I-40," advised Steve in the hospital room
after the whole thing was over. Through the sweaty
haze of panic, Jen's sleepy smile, the helium, pink balloon
inside his ribs, Dave could see the weight on his shy father —
who'd been known to pull loose teeth after swearing he wouldn't,
who fed secret bits of cheese to even the fattest dogs,
who'd named him David after God's own heart —
and he felt it on his own heart, handed down,
heavier than the thickest Bible in the house,
heavier than a case of beer, and he saw a little bit of it
rise off his own chest and settle like a crimson leaf
on Piney Creek on the crinkled forehead
of the nameless newborn in his arms.

Fundamentalist Sign Guys
on the Corner of West and Dickson

"The pleasures you seek are destroying your soul"
  has a pretty ring to it and sure enough,
I feel a twinge of shame, having just partaken
      in a heavy pour
of something heady and weighing
  the temptation of another. Bless my Baptist

heart which thrills at "Fear Jesus"—
  here is something I am doing right,
"fear" being mild for the notion that I can't
      go back to Yellowstone,
where the crust thins, for I'd fall in,
  be burned to nothing but a finger bone

the earth spits back. "A fiery end waits
  for those who won't repent," old news by now,
is just another mark I carry like the ping pong
      ball of scar tissue
in the small of my back from falling off a tire
  swing and landing on a pointy rock.

I love to drink, I love this place, its bars,
  its faces, briar glades and copperheads
and ticks; I love the lines of mountains,
      in debt to no progenitor
besides their own insistence that they stay, and I love
  every lonely man who's lain beside me,

yes, every blessed gasp. Damned
  by these and all the gifts of sense that swell
and break the heart like a wave that
      fills your mouth with salt
and sand, I'm a glutton for my mother's sorrow,
  her prayers abashing me from east to west,

back to Arkansas again, where Jesus lives and
  watches from the sober faces of the overalled
and bearded men so kindly come on Friday night
      bearing signs to warn me.

Teeth

Steve said, "I have always had remarkable teeth. Talked-about
teeth, wondered-at, the few times your ma sent me to the dentist;
straight across the front and white, though I chewed awhile
years back, still white as the underside of a deer's tail,
and never chipped, not even that time Bill knocked me out at Edna's.
You remember the other night, when it thundered like a gun
and we thought we might should head for the cellar?
Well, I'd been outside talking as I watered after supper,
praying you might say, more like blistering the Almighty
for all I thought He could yet do for me.
I'm tired of these same lessons, Lord, I said, *these same hard clocks
in the teeth, feels like waking up as a boy every damn day for forty years!*
I was steaming and splashing that hose all over, hitting the leaves
like I told you not to and stomping on the peas. Wasn't too long
before those clouds blew right over the top of us,
the lightning started streaking down over toward Chessmond's
and I got scared, just knowing I'd brought down judgment
on my arrogance and got you all in the way,
sure He was just about to turn me on my ear.
But all we got was a little shower and an awful noise as if to say,
a man with perfect teeth ought not to ask for more."

Chore

Dave was digging a ditch for Steve
and came across a corroded copper
belt buckle burrowed in the dirt;
he heard it *ting* when he touched it with the tip
of his shovel. Surely the quick shot
of adrenaline driving down his chest
was superstition instead of a spirit,
but he would've walked away if not
for Steve's inevitable stony stare
at supper for failing to finish the furrow.
John Gentry, a known jokester,
had recounted encounters with countless
hants who harrowed him in corners
of the wild, wooded waysides of Gorby,
and Dave could never divine the distance
between truth and clamor of nightbirds clawing
in John's tall tales. Crossing the pasture,
he eyed the woods, suffering perils
cloaked in bracken, brutal boars of the dark.

Paternoster

What I heard was crickets, frogs and crickets,
and your milk cow bawling for your hands,
and what I fear is that my heart buzzed up then
like a yellow jacket from those blooms
and departed your house forever.

I'd lain myself down in your blackberry rows,
but it's not our family way to go looking
when someone's wandered off,
as your father used to do right at suppertime.
You're the only one supper waits for now.

I know that you too have prostrated yourself,
one ear to the ground, one to the sky,
and waited for a word that doesn't come.
Faith, the thinnest of walls between us,
means every night at sundown you return

and your boots leave tracks of mud on the boards
beneath your chair at the head of the table,
while I fly far over the graying hills, sheltering
in caves and stream beds that echo endlessly
with a voice that I can't tell from yours.

A Close Call

Steve said, "I've not encountered many spirits here,
but John Gentry tells of a time when one
barreled out and barely missed him.
He headed up with his shovel and his ax
to dig for lead he heard was on his place,
and sure enough he found it, that metal detector
screeching like a cat on fire over
a sunk-in spot in the glade, so he set in.
When he stopped to drink some tea,
here it come sudden out of the trees —
a paint horse, unsaddled, rushing him at a hard gallop!
Only checked at the last. 'Didn't make a sound' he said.
'And nothing stirred around it.
In its eyes I saw it was a warning.'
He took off so fast he left his shovel
standing in the dirt. Don't go digging that ore, son,
nor the story that goes with it. Korea missed me
by the same hair that Indian ghost horse missed John."

The Last Earnest Prayer

I'd like to buy a little more of what it was
at work that January day when Dad was burning
brush for Nadine midway up her driveway,
Annie and I were setting the tips of sticks
on fire, and a copperhead began easing his way out
from a thick section of pine bark, woken
from his winter sleep by warmth, now
curling clockwise round the trunk not two feet,
no, not a snake's length from my head.
If there's anything left of what kept him addled,
what made me turn, a shot-glassful of grace
I haven't yet used up, let it snow down now
and melt in little dewdrops on my back
and save my life this one last time,
and I vow from now on I'll be good,
will let my hair grow long, the chords
of my throat rust, will never toss
a penny in a pond again. I'll be like
Nadine, who long since left this world,
praying in that ringing shack of a church,
Thank you for the pretty sunshine outside,
and thank you for the rain when it comes.

Humility

Steve said, "Farming will make a fool
of a man, pitting him against the likes of grass
and flies, creation's dimmest devils. Why,
it's an honor when a fox starts stealing chickens:
gives you something almost worth fighting against!
We got tater bugs in the apple roots,
Bermuda shoots choking every last vine
and only so much rain to go around.
Lo, there's that *chip-witter-witter* again,
warble of the whippoorwill perched
on the ridge of the roof of my heart.
But it's the thieving crow who cuts in furthest,
nesting in the tenderest spot, his hungry caws
scratching forth from my own hungry throat."

Mount of Olives

Blessed are the gentle, for they shall inherit the earth.
Matthew 5:5

My mother's hair is longer now than mine
and graying fast as if it waited till
she let it grow to loose its true nature
which is wise and of the moon,
though I have spent so long trying to cast her
off along with all the chores she brought me up
to do, how to scrub and cook and mend
and tend to men it seemed to me, instead
wanting always to be like the men, dirty-
fingernailed and intemperate, vociferous
with supper-table platitudes, she meanwhile
still at the stove frying up the last of whatever
we've already started eating,
but yesterday she told me she'd never climbed
Mount Olive, named for that biblical
epicenter of the divine, and thought
she'd walk it come spring to see
if she could hear anything,
and now I'm asking too
if all her years of straining
milk and kneading bread and wearing
down the path to the garden to gather
cucumbers, corn, greens whose seeds
she dried and saved in paper bags, all
those hours sitting silent in the dark
like a stone set on top of another stone
by someone's hand a hundred years
ago on the very hill passed down
from her own mother, waiting for the Lord
to speak — and I can't say if sometimes He
did or does — every card she's sent
to every distant place I've gone, on which are drawn
lumpy hens, my father as a stick-man with a bucket,
and written scraps of Psalms to stoke
my heart even in doubt, if all the quart jars
I've emptied of tomatoes and taken back home
she's washed and refilled, resealed, every hog
she's watched die snorting then boiled
its outer layers for lard, and all the well-earned
bites of all the simple meals blessed
by my father's tested supplication
at their fine oak table will amount to
anything in me that when someone someday,
friend or child or man or God forbid, herself
hungry, blue, in need of something leavened
comes to me, will rise to that occasion and give,
of my own two hands, all I know how to give.

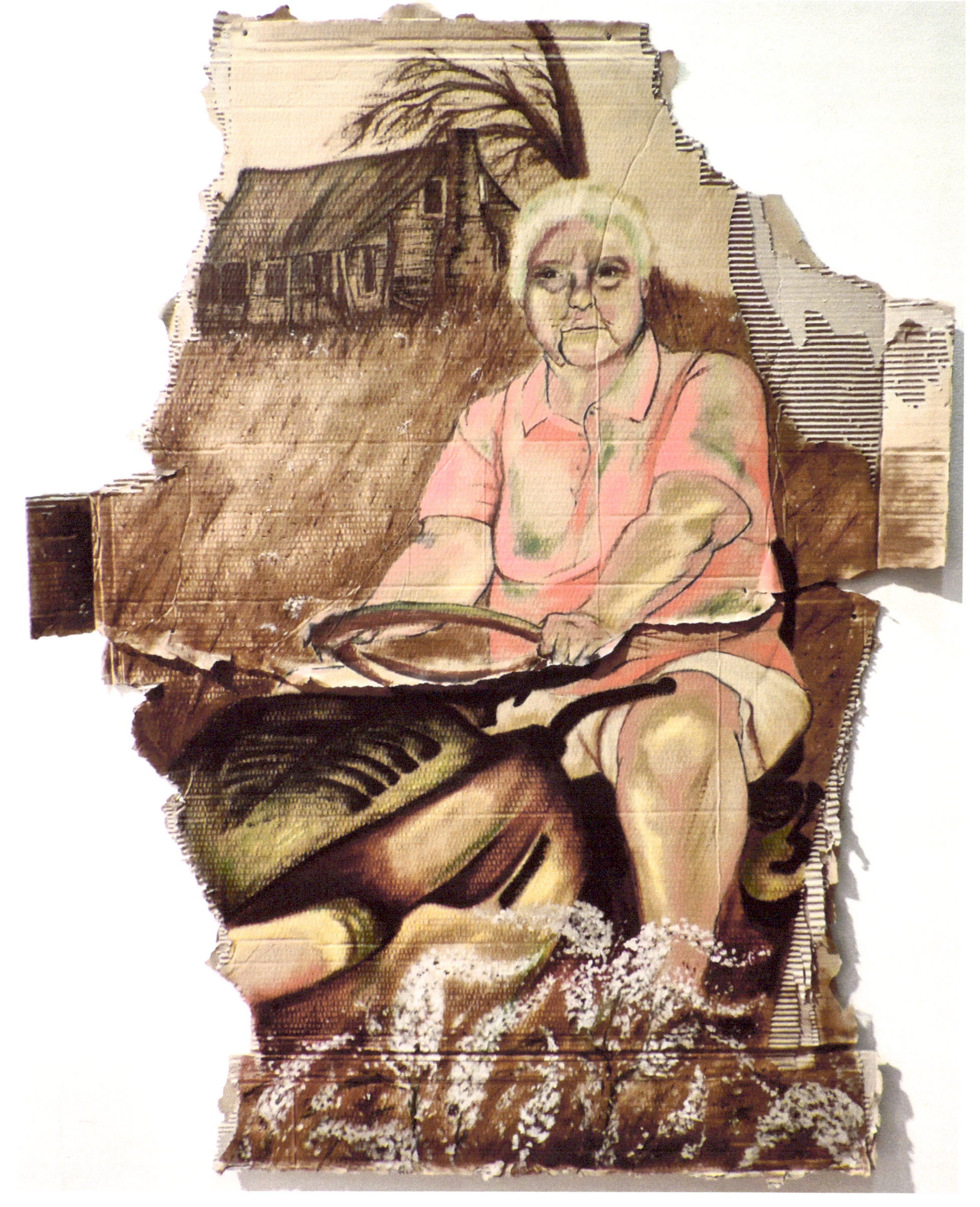

CHELSEY BECKER
My Black Cohosh

My Granny is from rural Arkansas and knew from a young age that she was gay. However, she married a man and had five children due to societal pressure. In "My Black Cohosh," Granny rides her mower over black cohosh flowers continually while her house deteriorates in the background. Black cohosh was used by the Cherokee to help with menstrual pain in small doses and abortion in larger doses. In this piece, cohosh represents her struggle with gender expectations while also identifying her own definition of femininity. This lifelong struggle has caused other parts of her life to be neglected. This piece is painted with oil paint on found cardboard, representing the fragility of the story and how it otherwise would have been forgotten.

SAIRA KHAN
Bird Girl

I.

A small child,
wide-eyed, starry-browed,
places her thumb against her lips;
Reconsiders.
She tugs at the fingers in her free hand,
Brown, curious, creeping caterpillars.
The checkout clerk smiles.
Her eyes don't form wrinkles,
"Well aren't ya the cutest thing?"

My mother laughed and said thank you.
When we left, I turned and watched the clerk,
briskly wiping the memory on her apron.

II.

In the beginning,
God expects a name,
The name whispered by angels,
Perfect little things.

On the first day of school,
little round eyes gleam,
tiny hands clutch new weapons—
pencil and eraser—
one to create and the other to forget,
both necessary.

A teacher mispronounces.
A shy little girl stays silent.

On the first day of a new year,
twelve years later,
a teenager corrects the teacher.
Her classmates squabble,
the chatter of excited squirrels.

She says her real name aloud and believes it today.

III.

I liked a boy. He was bland and wore his
name like a crown. I felt my head bow when
he walked past.

One day I grew a voice that slithered and
shook in my chest. The brave snake enliv-
ened my small feet, soggy in dirty white
sneakers because I peddled in the rain.

I stood on his porch. His father raised his
eyebrows and talked in a hushed voice. Yes,
he was home. Yes, he would get him. I stood
there shivering on the outside, giggling on
the inside, never invited in.

IV.

My feet collided into a wall,
and just through the threshold, in the foyer,
entered another world.

I loved my neighbor for her mom,
that I felt forty at fifteen.
The house I left faded and this new one
grew cheerier, casseroles and Christmas trees.

Then I met the grandmother.
Her polished red fingernails and dark pink lips
discussed my arrivals, exchanged notes,
privileged appendages.

Days later, the luster had dimmed.
I watched fat droplets slide down my window.

What nice skin I have.
What white teeth.

V.

“What do you believe?”

“In God.”

“*No*, what do you *really* believe?”

In God I trusted, but they didn’t trust me.
Two freckled faces cornered me by the Coke machine,
their cheeks growing more colorful as they spoke.
I insisted and they persisted
to remind me “my God” is not theirs.

In a way, I hoped they were right.
“My God” would have just chuckled anyway.

VI.

Dear Daughter,

I am writing to you that I can begin to forget your face I never even saw. Your socks I’ll never fold. If you knew that I chose his socks over yours, that his socks needed to be around, whereas I just wanted to cradle your tiny cotton feet in my hands.

The rare warmth in his voice that day we discovered you, as if he knew he would end us.

His mother will never know. Mine will never forget.

I will see you when I look at the stars. I will swear I see your face as perfection, neither white nor brown.

VII.

Strong women carry buckets
and babies and burdens
up and down stairs and press
secrets into their daughters' ears.

How To Survive These Men in Our Houses;
the man you will love,
and then men whose eyes you avert on the street.

My mother carried and balanced the load. She learned the tricks,
stooped to whisper, "Get up Little One."

I sit surrounded by my words, my mishaps,
broken bones and plucked feathers,
loneliness and hunger:
scattered tools for a frenzy whose name means "Bird Girl."

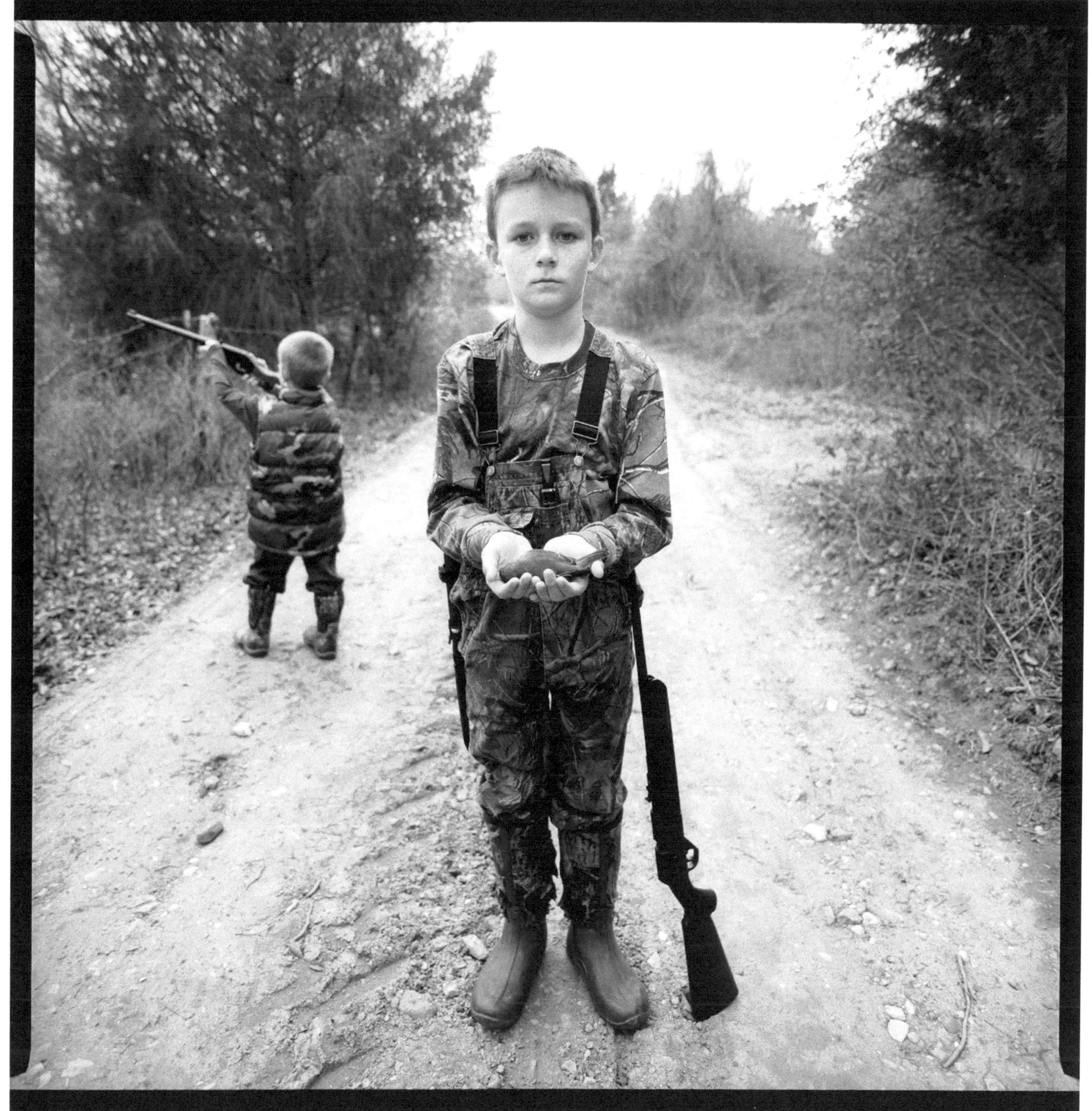

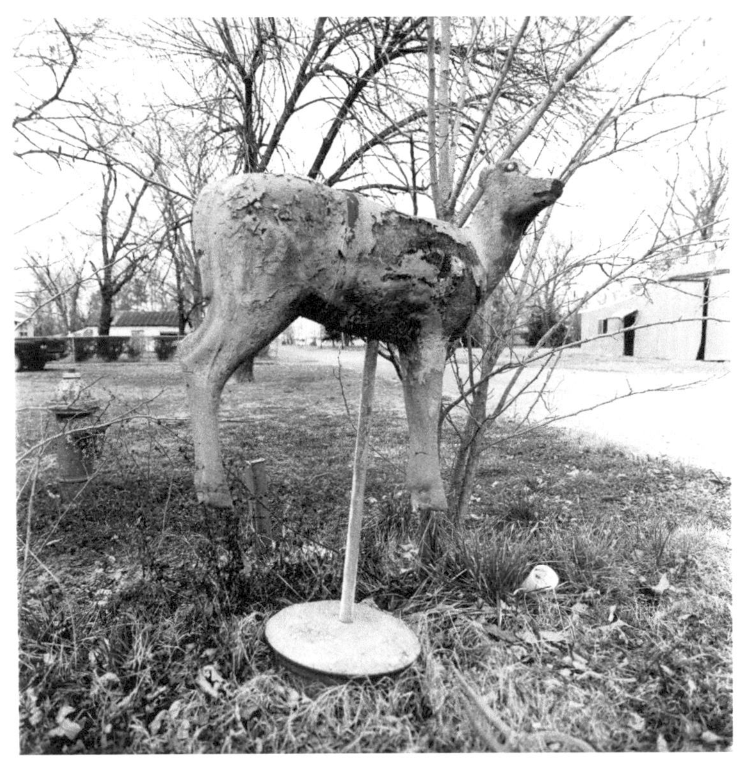

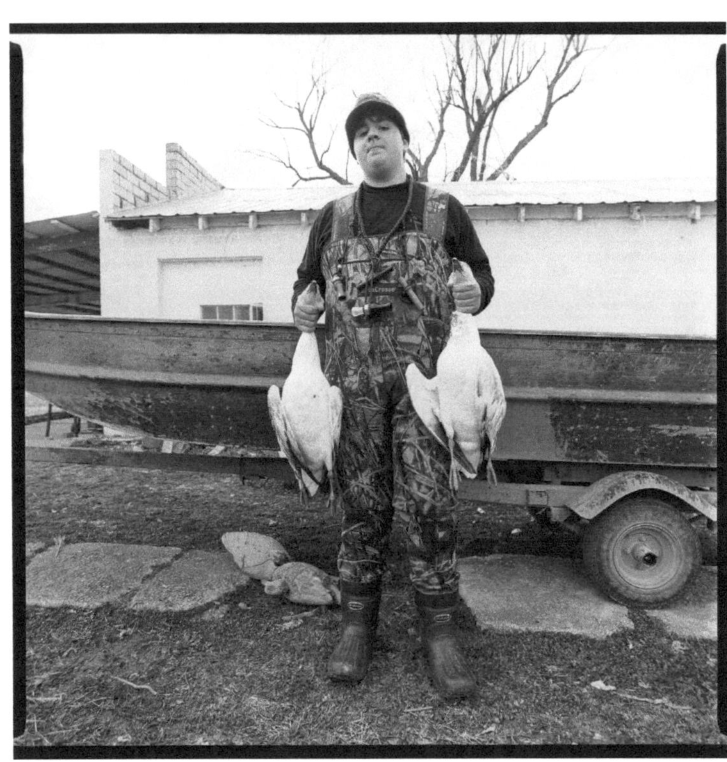

MAXINE PAYNE

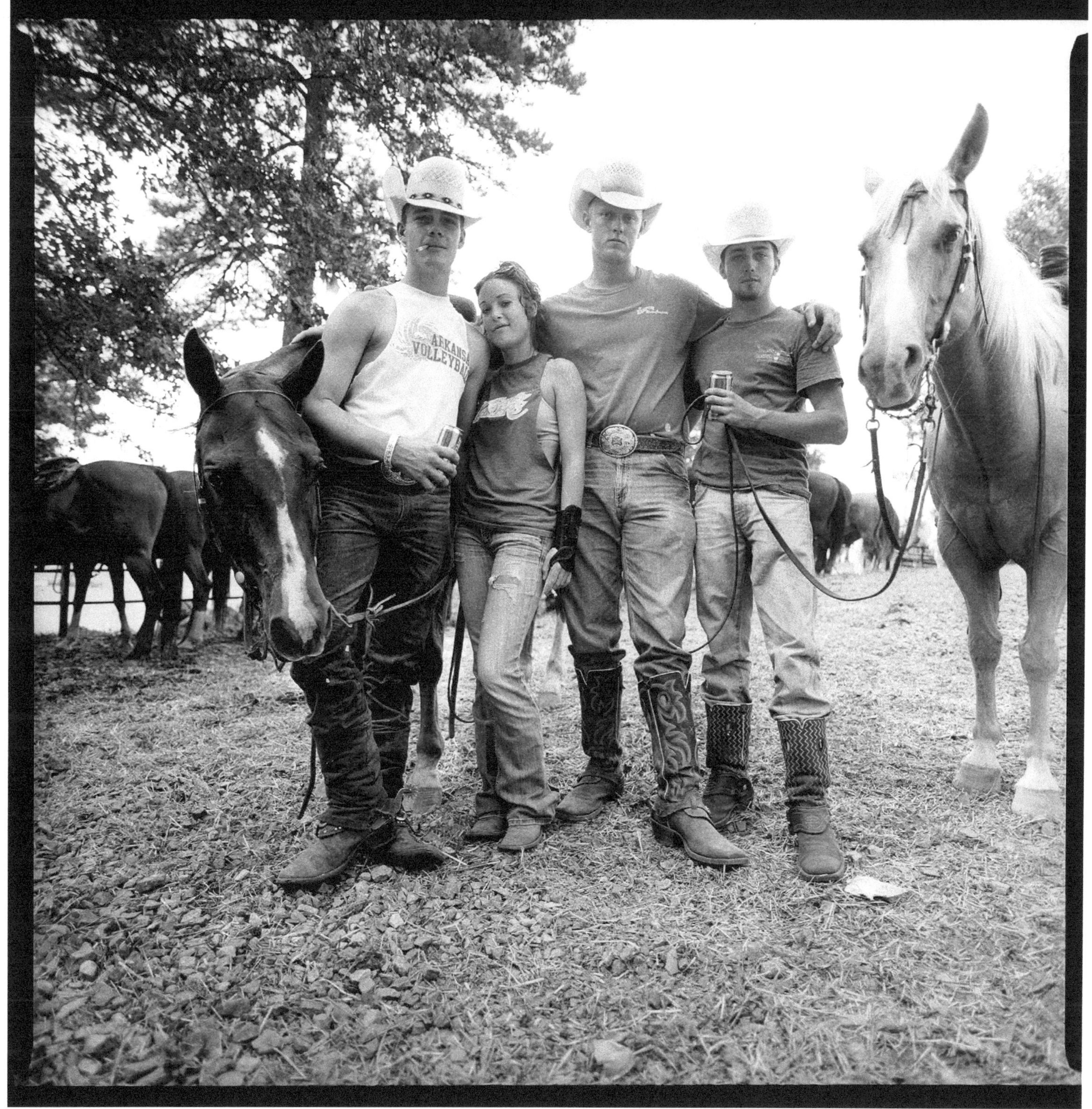
ARKANSA
VOLLEYBA

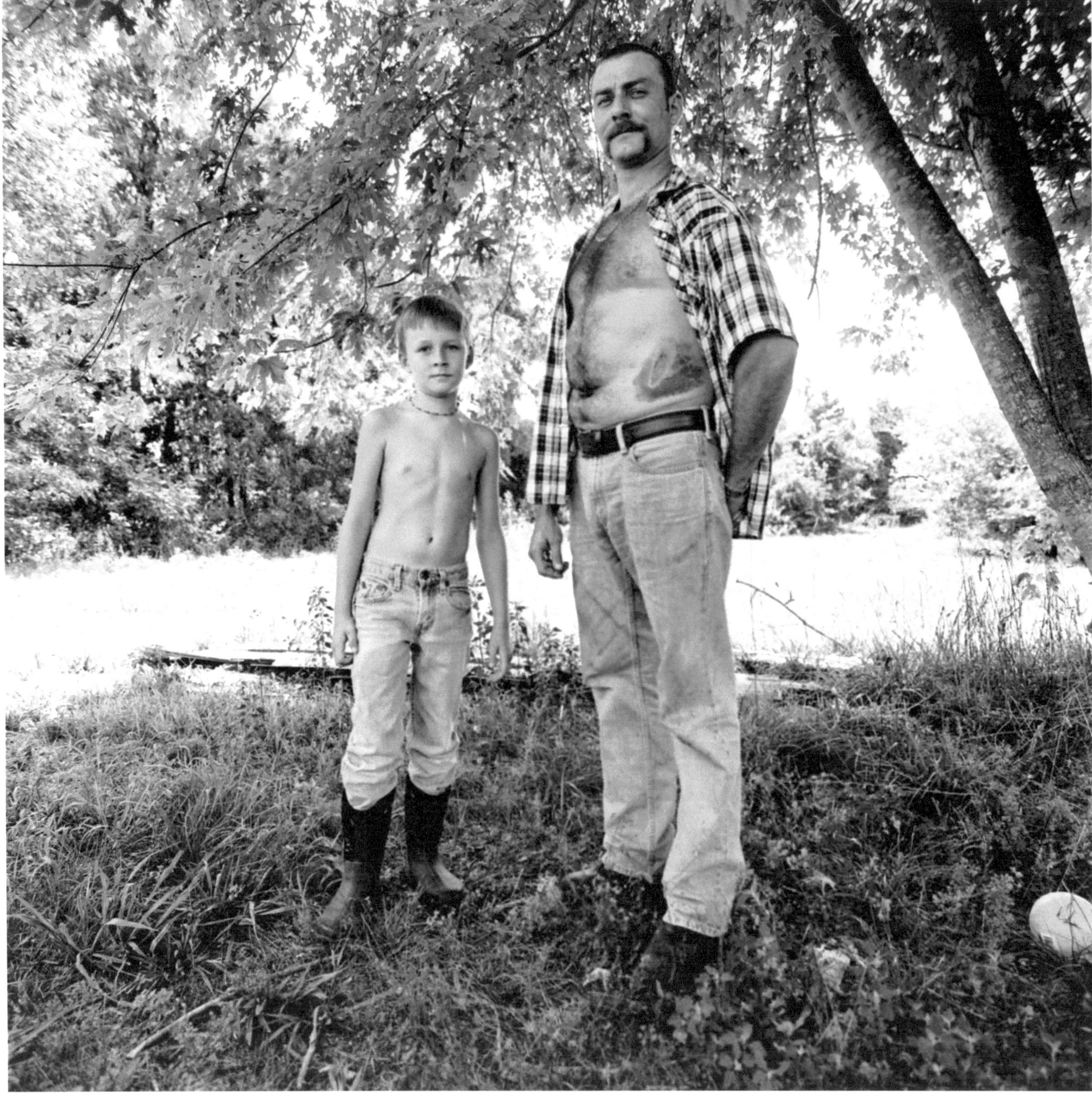

ED MADDEN

When I was a young animal

When I was a young animal.
I learned by watching others,
my father and the other men,
my mother, closing the door.

The field smelled like a field.
I didn't know that then.
I could smell my young uncle
on his hand-me-down shirts
and pants, the buckskin coat
with fringed sleeves, smell
my grandmother's home
when I tugged him over me,
my young uncle, the one
who showed me his dad's magazine.

On the farm, we were a pack,
the other cubs and me,
roaming the dirt roads and fields,
slinging clods at cars
and one another, pissing
on anything, into the fire
they built behind the shop
to burn the trash, the small
cans exploding in the flames.
We were sunburnt, chigger-bit,
our mothers checked our skin
for ringworm and ticks.
I was a young animal,
I learned by watching others.

Country of Origin

In your father's country, machines comb the fields, the men smoking in the twilight. The air smells of exhaustion. Sunset is a glowing butt your dad tosses from his truck. Something's left undone. The world wants to touch you, the leaves, the flowers lifting. The world doesn't believe you.

In your mother's country, everyone has two jobs, or three. The year is measured in fists of flowers in a jar. Everyone loses something. When you slip on your mother's blue nightgown, blue and white, you are briefly a woman, but you are not.

Or he is not. Or I am not. Or they are not.

In this country, we are eight or nine. There is no such thing as time.

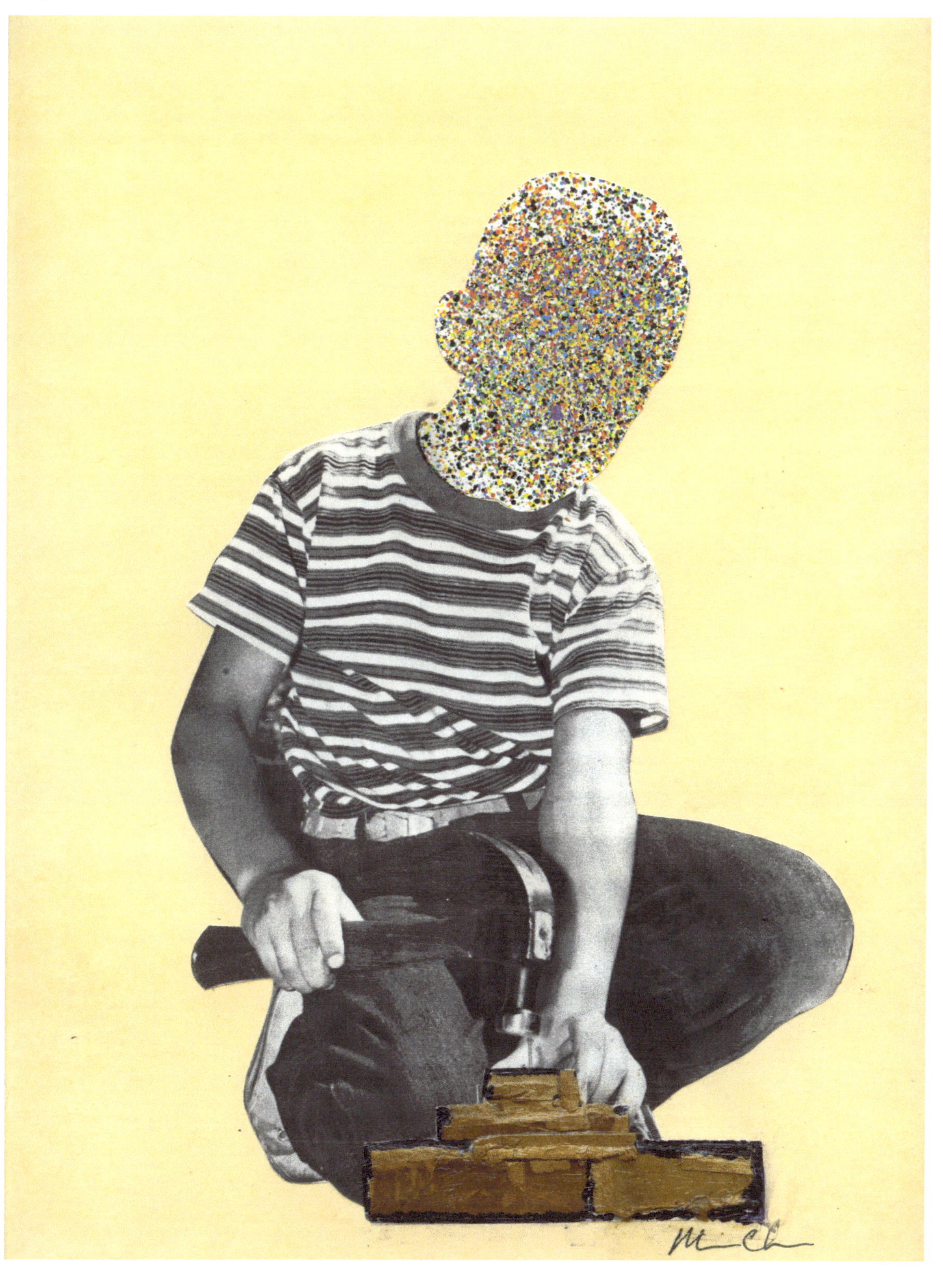

MEIKEL CHURCH

Assemblage

JUSTIN BOOTH

Before

Before I was
another pony-tailed
old man in sandals
at the grocery
on Saturday mornings
talking too loud
to Merry
about Austin and
how much better
it used to be
to live there,
Before I was
a big deal in Little Rock,
her darling drunken poet—
western style jackets
and jokes and schtick
of the sad clown's lot
and hashtags and
the luckiest man,
Before I slept on
sidewalks and shot dope
and stole Chore Boy
screens to rebuild
a glass rocket to
numbing and dumbing
and making
my thoughts mute,
Before I served time
in prisons and jails for
offending the dignity
of Arkansas laws,
before I ate spreads
of ramen and Cheetos
and lit cigarettes from
outlets high up
on the wall behind the TV,
Before the wives and
the others, the women
who loved me,
before two daughters
and a son with my chin
before I was a bricklayer
practicing a trade,
all bent-over back,
sweat in my eyes
and hands as rough
as sandpaper,
Before college
late to the show
and Bukowski,
Raymond Carver, and
a Cummings tattoo
on Harry Crews' arm,
before falling in love,
Before California,
and St. Louis,
and Johnny Cash Sundays,
and another dead friend,
before overdosing and
high school and
derogatory names
and the rest so strange,
Before all of that
I was my mama's little boy,
and she'd sing me songs
then hum to me asleep
in the house my Grandpa built
in Milligan Ridge.

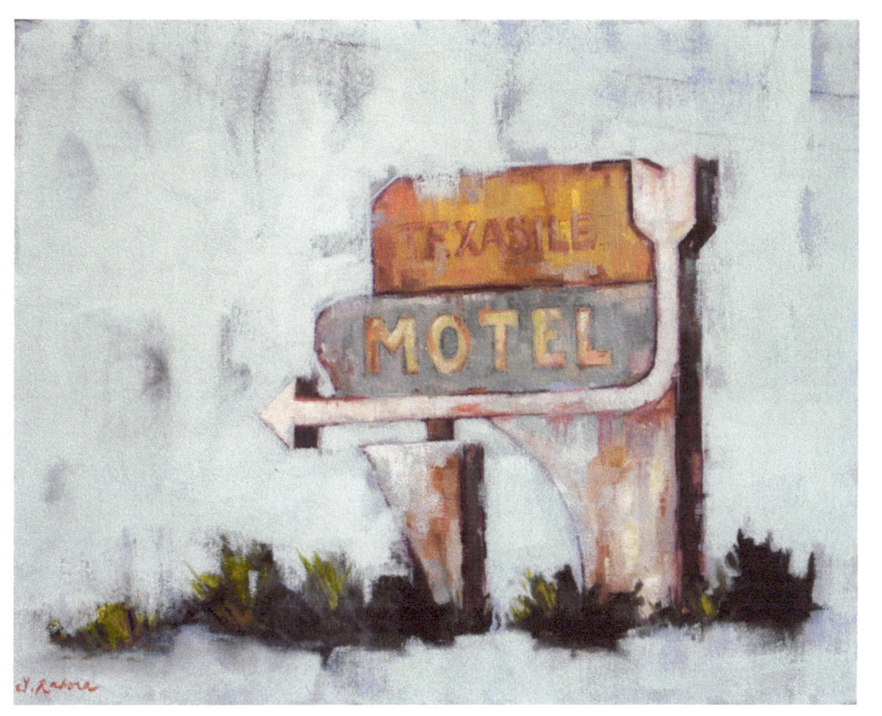
MOTEL

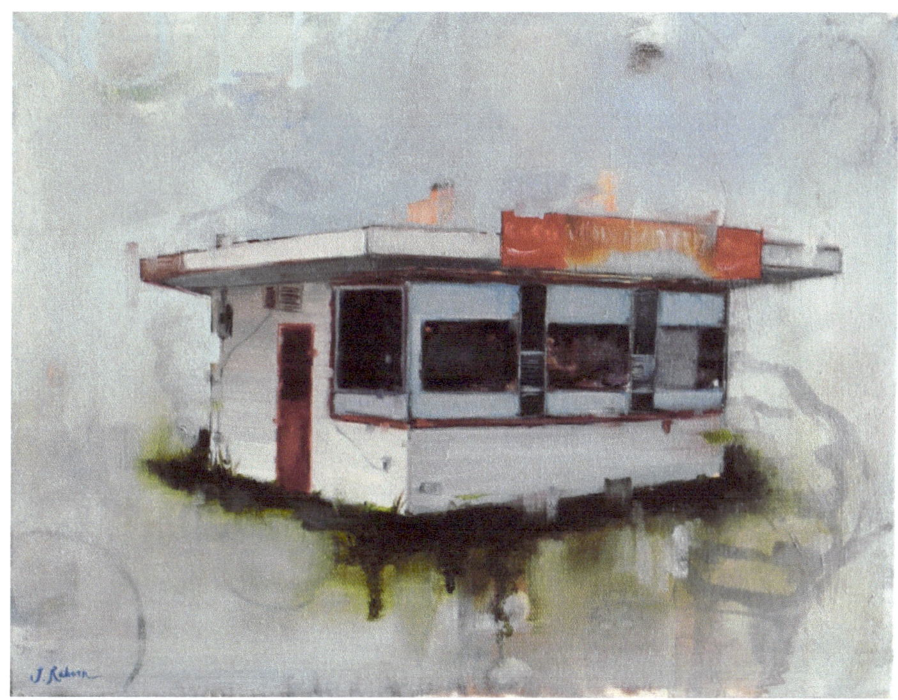

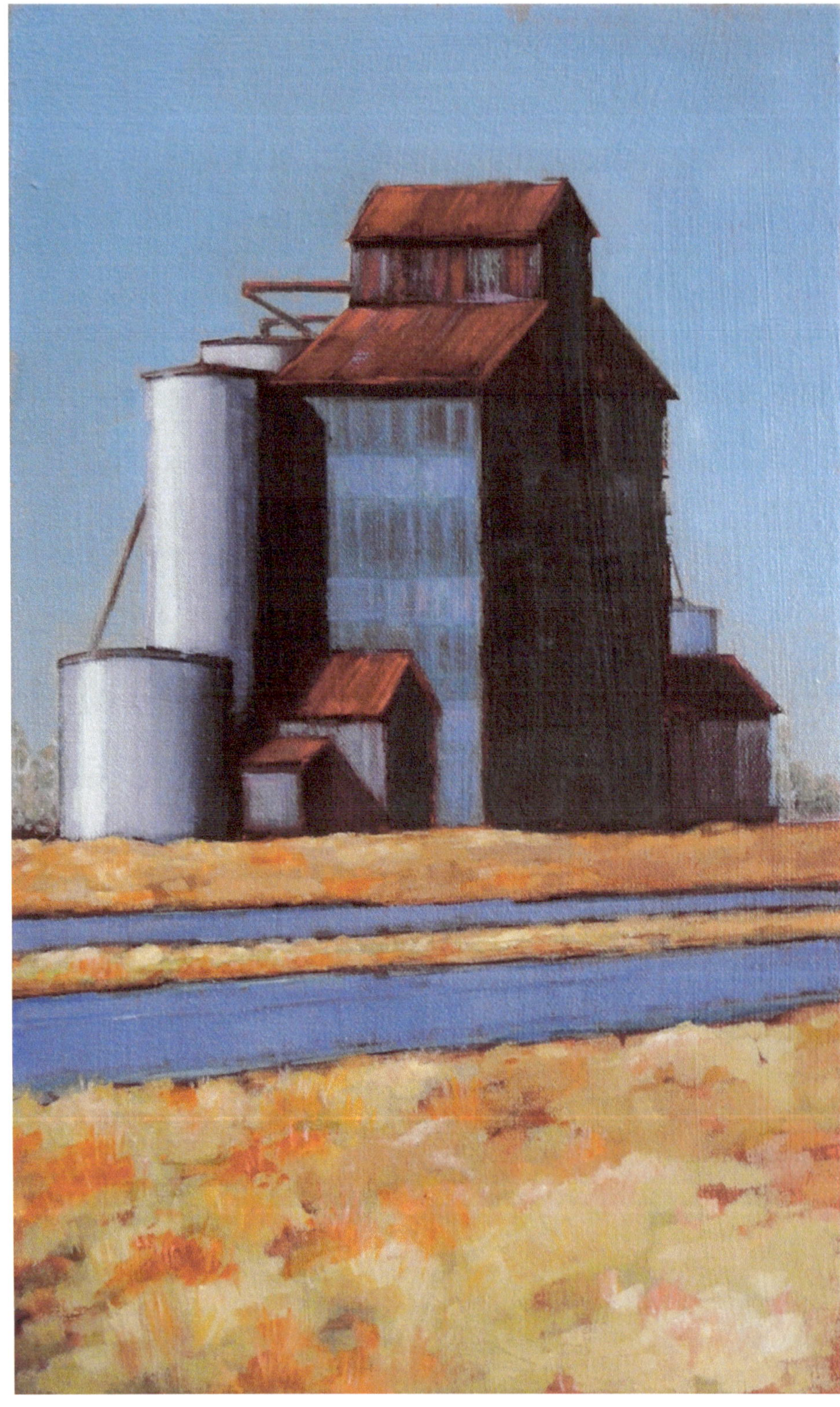

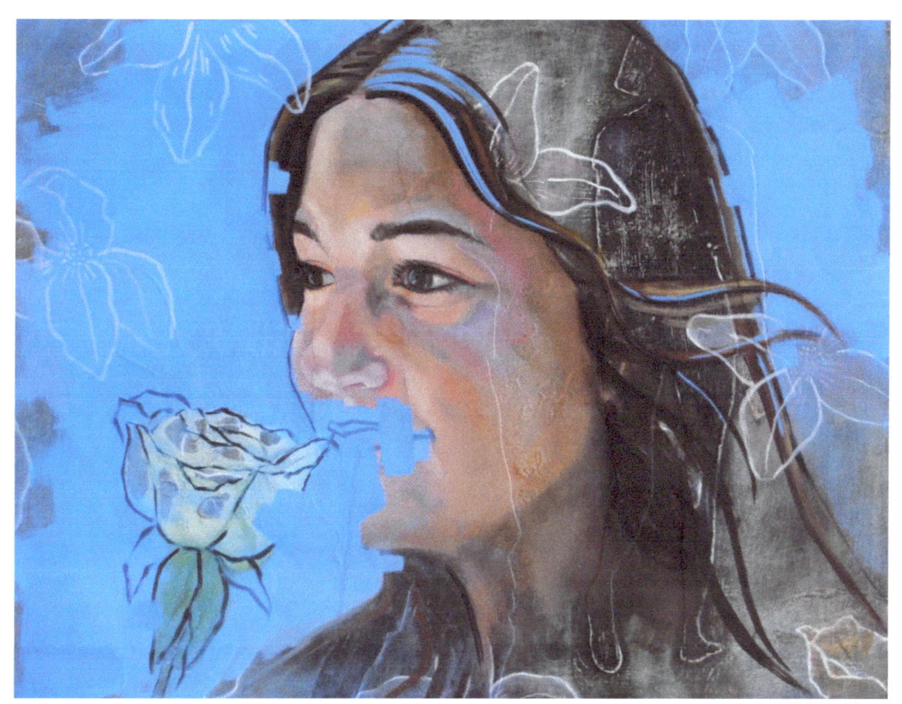

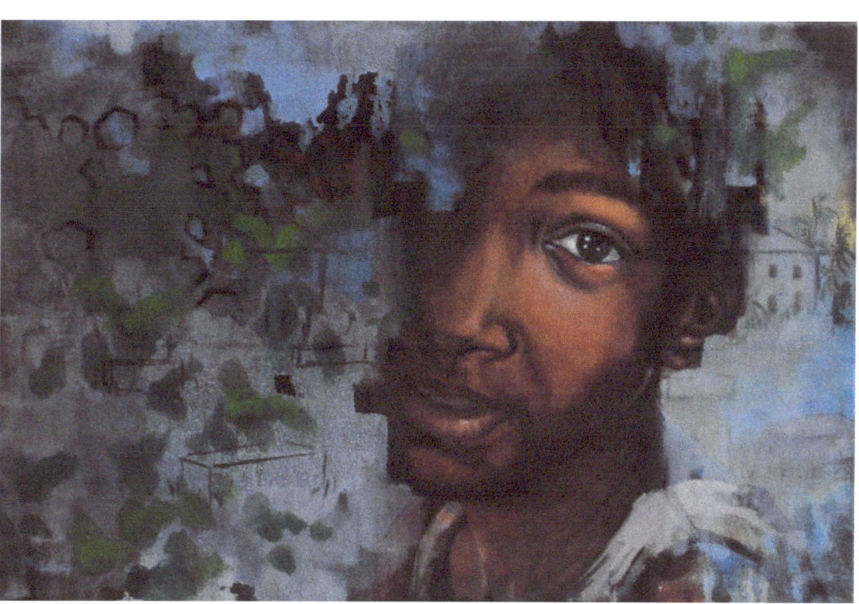

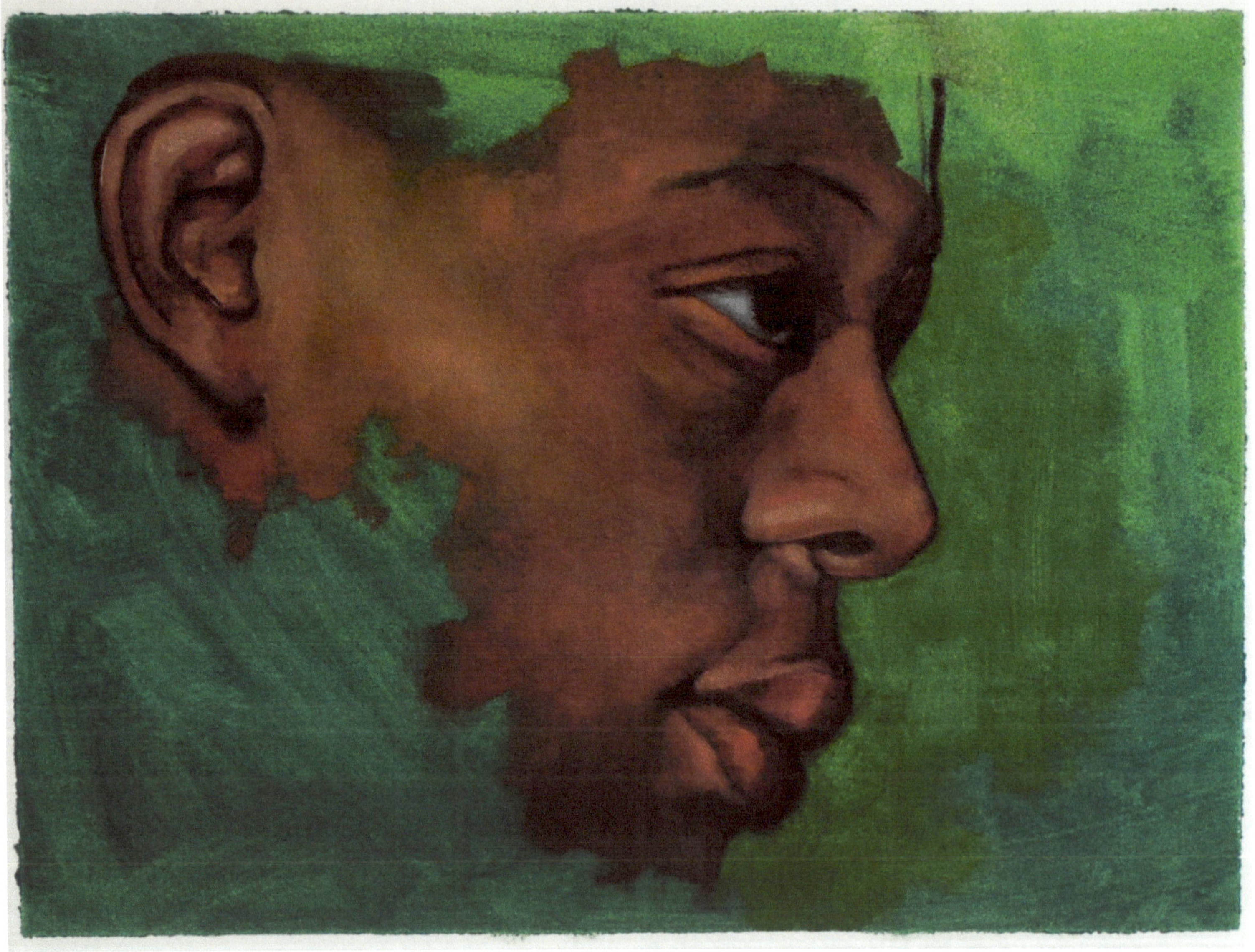

LAURA RABORN

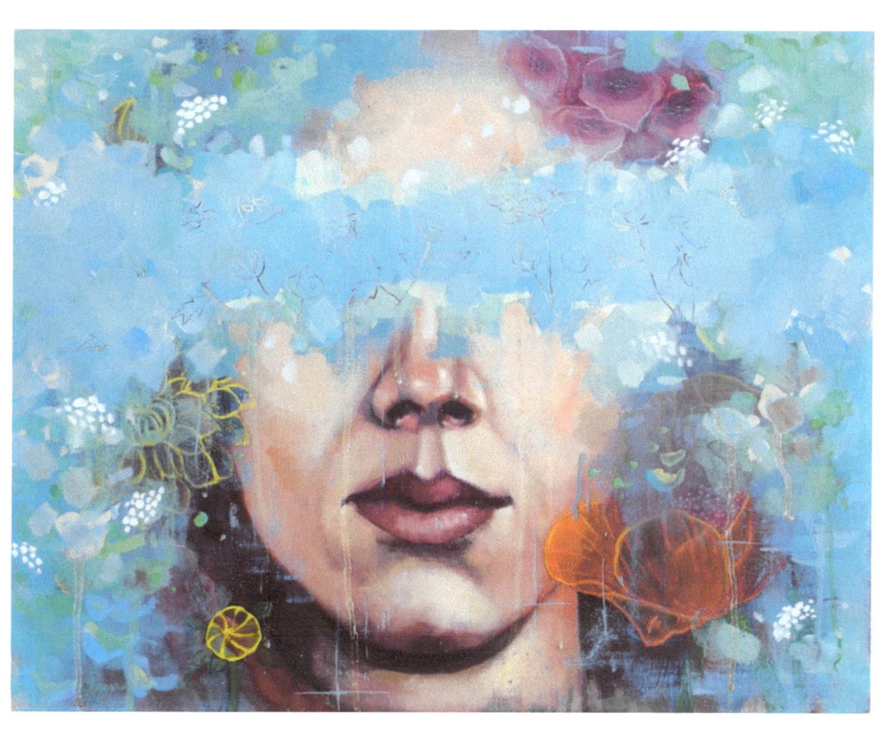

I was raised in Arkansas with the exception of 5 years when my dad served in the Navy and we moved around from coast to coast. My entire adult life, I have lived in Arkansas. With each passing year (and many have passed), my view of my home state shifts and fluctuates. At times I am proud of where I live. When judgment and intolerance surface, I am ashamed.

This awareness feeds my creative choices as I consider the general concept of each individual's unique perspective. Everything we see and every person we meet has a story unknown to us. If we could stop and truly see each other instead of making assumptions, I believe much needed understanding and healing could occur. With this in mind, I paint people as a way of stopping, noticing, and respecting each human. Similarly, I paint abandoned buildings as a way of honoring a history that is no longer visible but was perhaps once vibrant and important to someone. Slowing down to study people and places helps me avoid assumptions and teaches me to imagine a history beyond myself.

WENDY TAYLOR CARLISLE

Rumors

To write about Arkansas summer you have to have the animal memory of swelter, of low water, of dry sumps, of deer come close to the cow pond and cattle down to the licklog, of NO BURN signs. You have to remember 2012, the second hottest year on record or 1956, which by words of mouth was the first. But this summer I'm writing about was the worst summer since Satan fell or so we thought. The cities simmered to a boil in their knockout tarmac, bubbling down to heat stroke. Everywhere they preached
Armageddon like always. And like always they used 110 degrees for proof.

With no air condition, it was too hot to make love even with fans at the head and foot of the bed making a middle turbulence. We couldn't move after noon or sleep before midnight. How many hours can a person spend at Harts pushing a wire cart through the cans and bottles—15 minutes to choose a sponge, ½ hour for a soft drink that only stays chilled straight out of the cooler box? Winter was a rumor that summer as each scarp overheated. We searched for anything cold and hid what we found.

It may be that we were brown and swam it. It may be that when we could, we stepped down off the cliff into the icy river imagining ourselves Cherokee just passing through or Quapaw or settlers who learned long ago to make peace with the heat. Let's just say the weather sweated us and we got no relief from those jumped-up preachers.

"[D]own to the licklog" relates to an old rancher's trick. The second-to-last thing before cattle were slaughtered, a ranch hand took them first to a salt lick and then to water to increase their butchered weight.

BLOSSOM

...old in a blossoming earth Robert Creeley

In the south of my childhood, time passed
like a plate of fried chicken. Grandma made lard
biscuits, cooked rashers of bacon, fried pork
chops, presided over the hugging and sassing
and eating and telling and pulling of sticker burrs.

I looked to her for solace and solutions. She delivered
axioms and injunctions and was indifferent to the one
strong chin hair that grew and, when plucked,
grew back, unkillable as a cockroach. How and why
do someone's eyebrows grow both thin and wild?

In the south of my childhood we knew our place
And kept it until, like grandma's, our strength of hand
yielded to loss of grip as cans and silverware tumbled
away from us like petals from a blossoming branch.

In The Year of Our Lord

Things happen one after another. During the winter, Matt gets stuck at a four-blast crossing. The oncoming train gathers speed then squanders it. His death is weirder now than when it is happening. In spring, a journalist is fired for fabricating interviews with Sharon Stone and Brad Pitt. He defends himself by calling it "conceptual art." Late summer reaches us with its afternoon heat, brutal as a mishandled pit bull, with its Canada geese in an overhead flotilla. It lasts too long, a body blow of afternoon air, to settle on our shoulders like a hundred houseflies. In time, fall rain stones the cow pond. Don't leave the house then without a sweater, a patriotic conversation.

All year long, humans find courage in moonshine, spies offer sex for information and the town square's buildings teeter on the edge of disrepair. All year long, the unmasked leap up, battalions of flags and sweat sweep past. All year long when I try to talk about suffering, a caul is over the words, *bully* and *shove*. By December, I want whatever caresses me for need or pleasure. Who doesn't love a dark harbor?

6 Poems

Poem with Political Leanings
Things could have gone differently for the left, for the right,
for all of us humping our implausible lives
into an ideal future that appears preoccupied with theology and violence.
Nevertheless, rain clouds over the Ouachitas excel in not giving a shit,
nor do possums who, although they hiss, live in peace with their ticks.

Poem with Ecology
Something about maples. Something about coal slurry. Something about a stream
and what we are allowed to throw in.

Poem Awake at 2 AM
Night keeping company with a regulation moon.
Night in the unlit.
This time of night belongs to the field mice and packrats
and the cats who find them.

Poem with Magic
The saints and magicians trundle among us.
To steal from silence nothing silence misses.

Poem That Might be a Love Poem
The lie he said didn't matter
The lie that did was floorboards filled with rain,
furlongs, condoms, the lie was ornate
we ate that lie from each other's hands.

Poem with My Life Philosophy in It
I always think there is time for one more.

The Flavor of Pain

It was the middle of a winter night and the leaves had vanished from the front yard like soap from a hotel bathroom. It was that cold when she showed but we kept up a conversation we began decades before by the Arkansas River, summer talk that embraced a slide of light and reflected back two kinds of hoodoo affection. Older than me, she never admitted her age. As for the kids, she was ahead in girls but she never held me up. She said, "Boys. You know how they are, they don't bleed." On that we agreed.

This particular night she came in like a small dog. A small dog is a hand mirror, a pocket-handkerchief. You can bully a small dog. When small dogs soil the rug it is a tiny dark stain, when they vomit it is a Lilliputian heap. Like any little pooch she smelled of compost and the circus, sawdust and a surfeit of dung. It's funny how lost feelings appeared then, rising up like roach parts in a spice jar, like a dead ant from the bottom of a glass of beer. I loved her that night as I did before so when she said "...sure I was raped but everybody is," I applauded her nerve. Even as a dog, she contained multitudes.

Her presence was a poultice on a septic wound. Her presence demanded I never say, "I told you so." Or "Yes. I knew." In her presence, I had to shut it. I had to listen as the sun cleared the gully—oak and pine and dogwood. I had to be still as the sycamores sketched themselves in black and brown against what was left of the snow that clung to the rocks like bad memories, like mud on the shoes of a hunter. I had to ignore the small red bird of her cigarette against the brush and the occasional neighborhood gunshot, and when she left, I had to boil that bone for its salt taste. I had to simmer her story for the flavor of her pain.

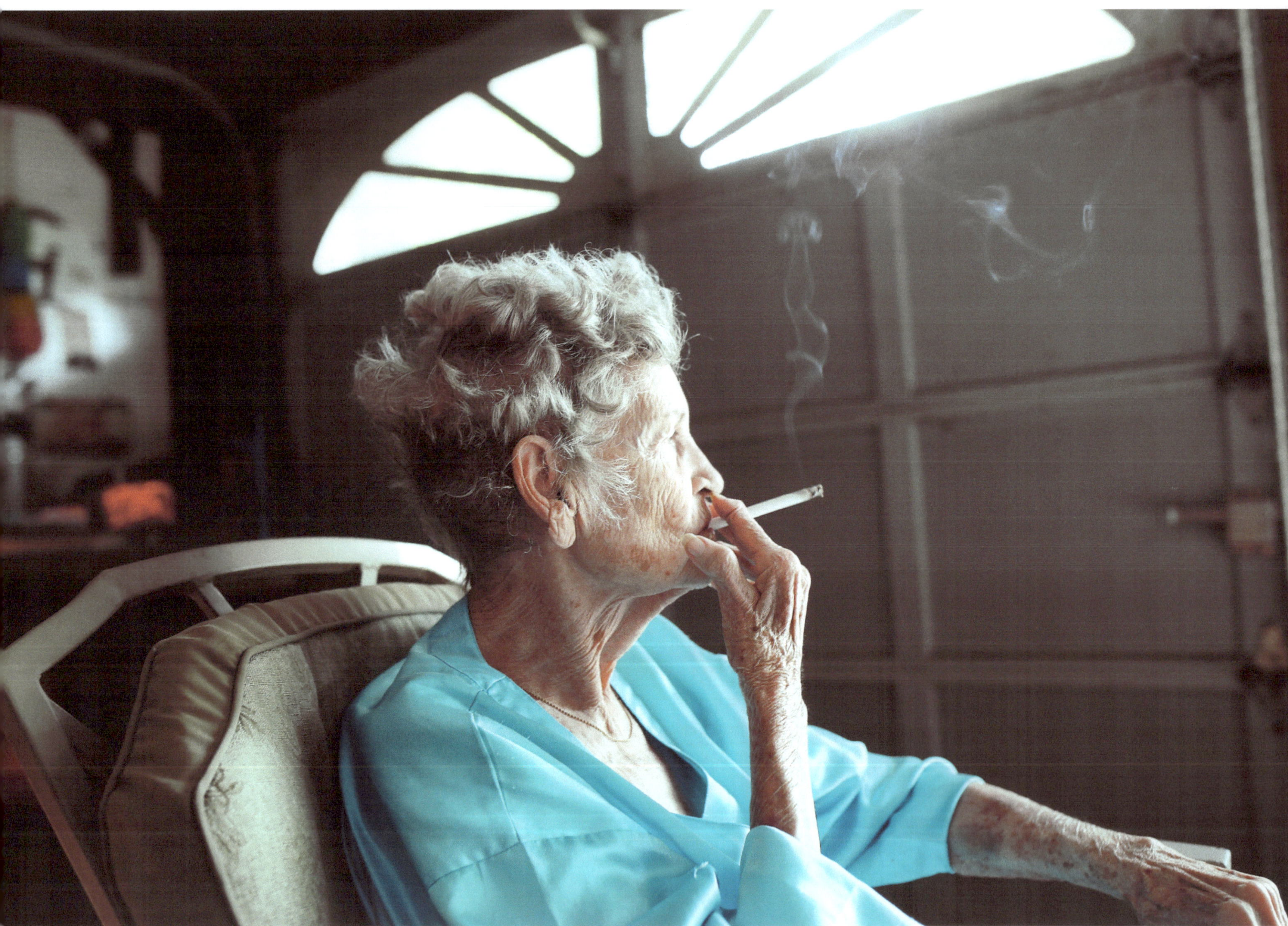

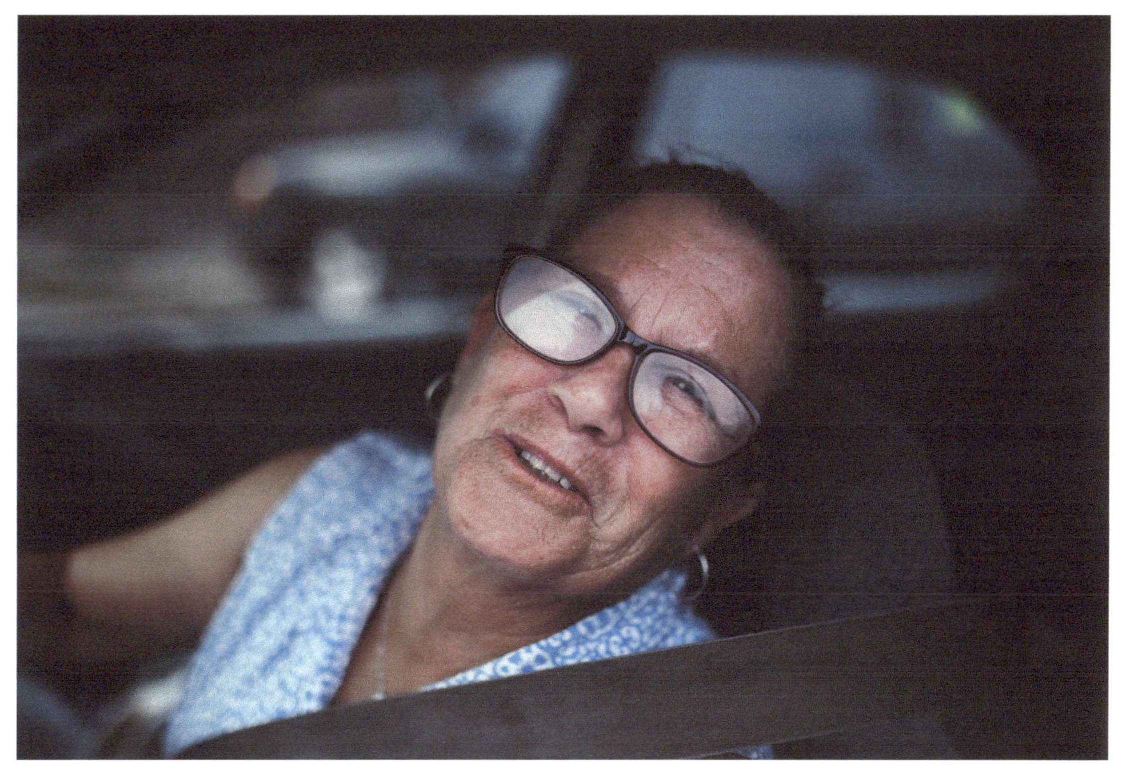

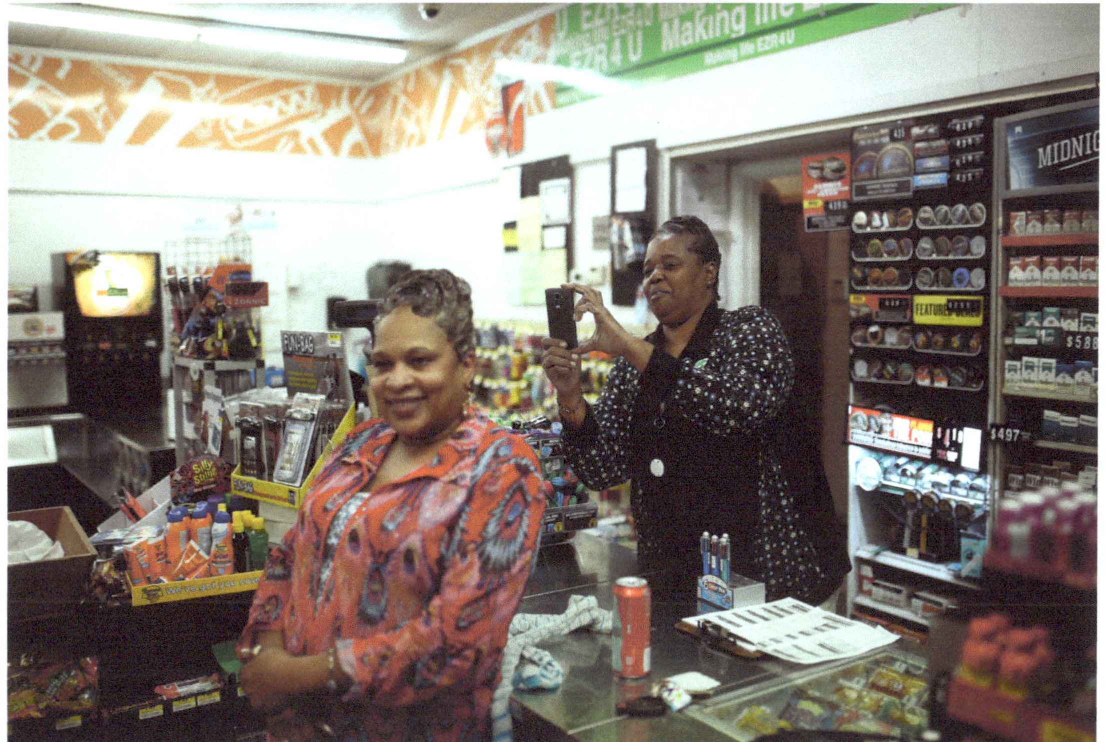

MATT WHITE
Strangers Along the Way

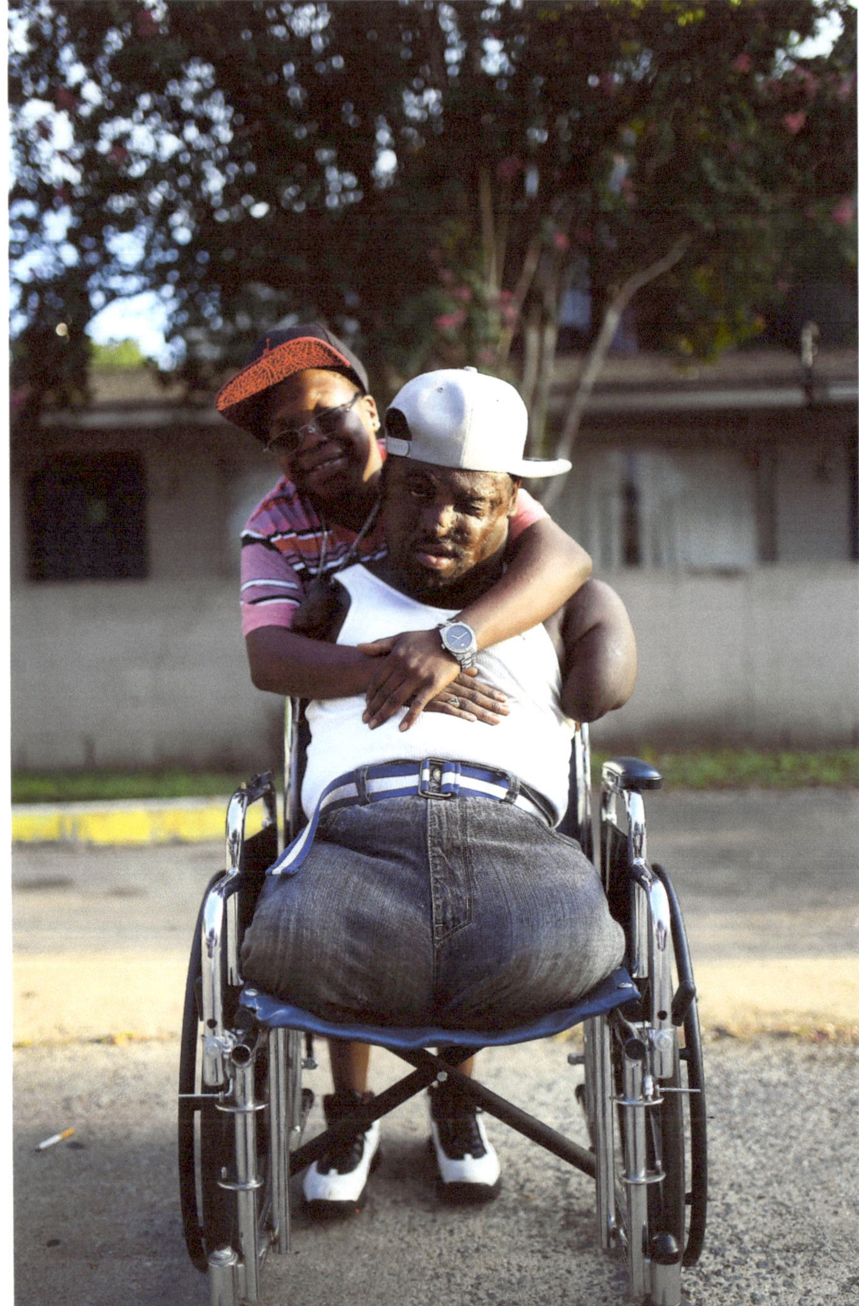

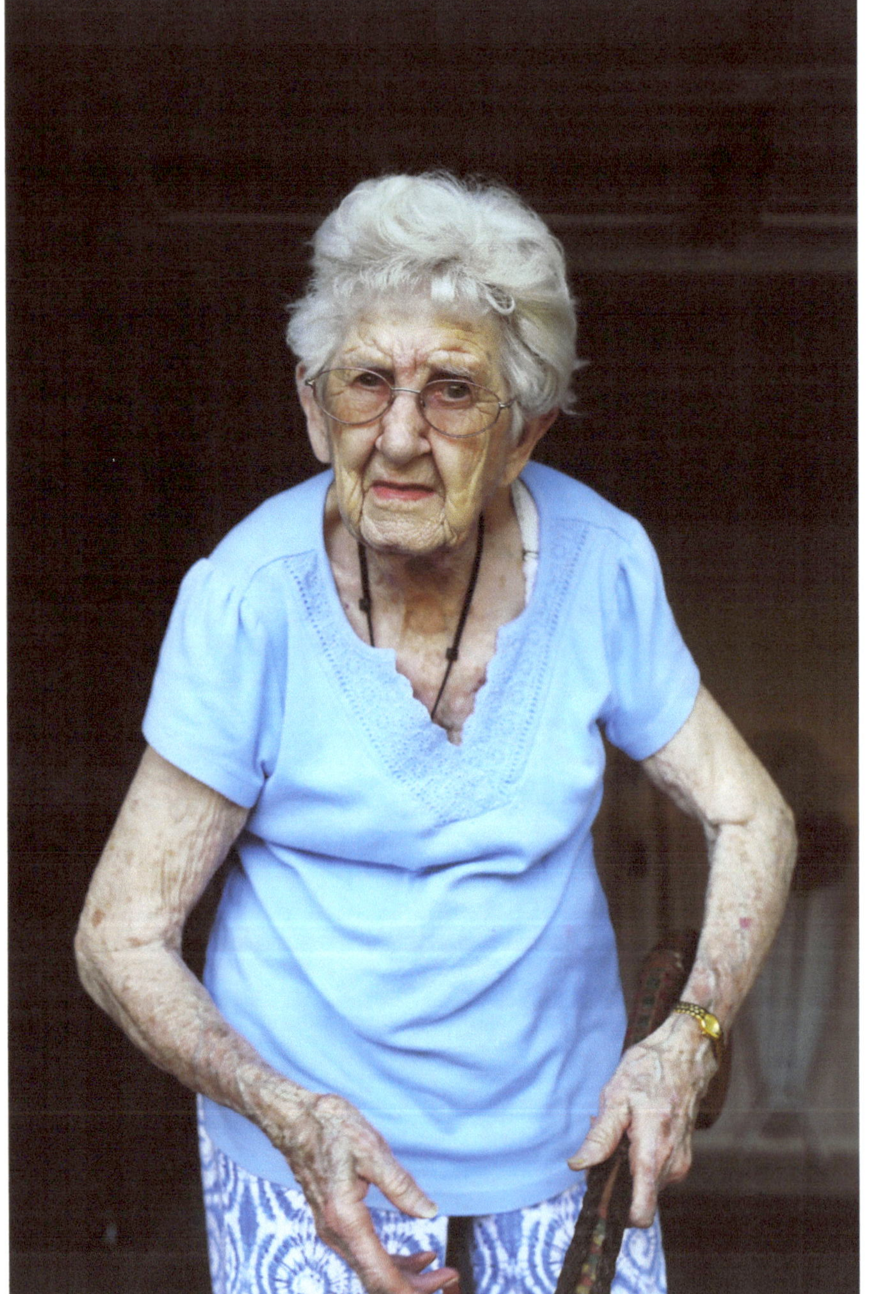

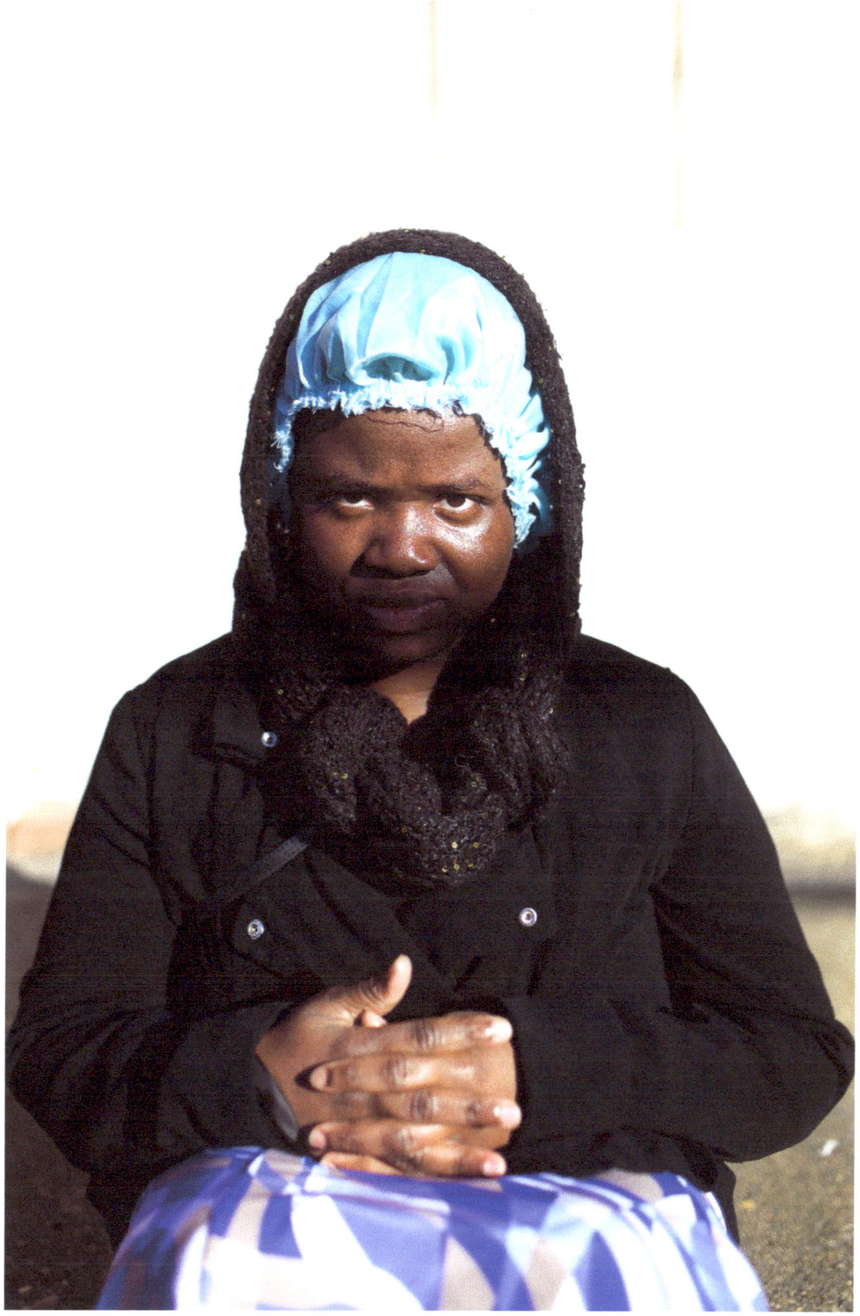

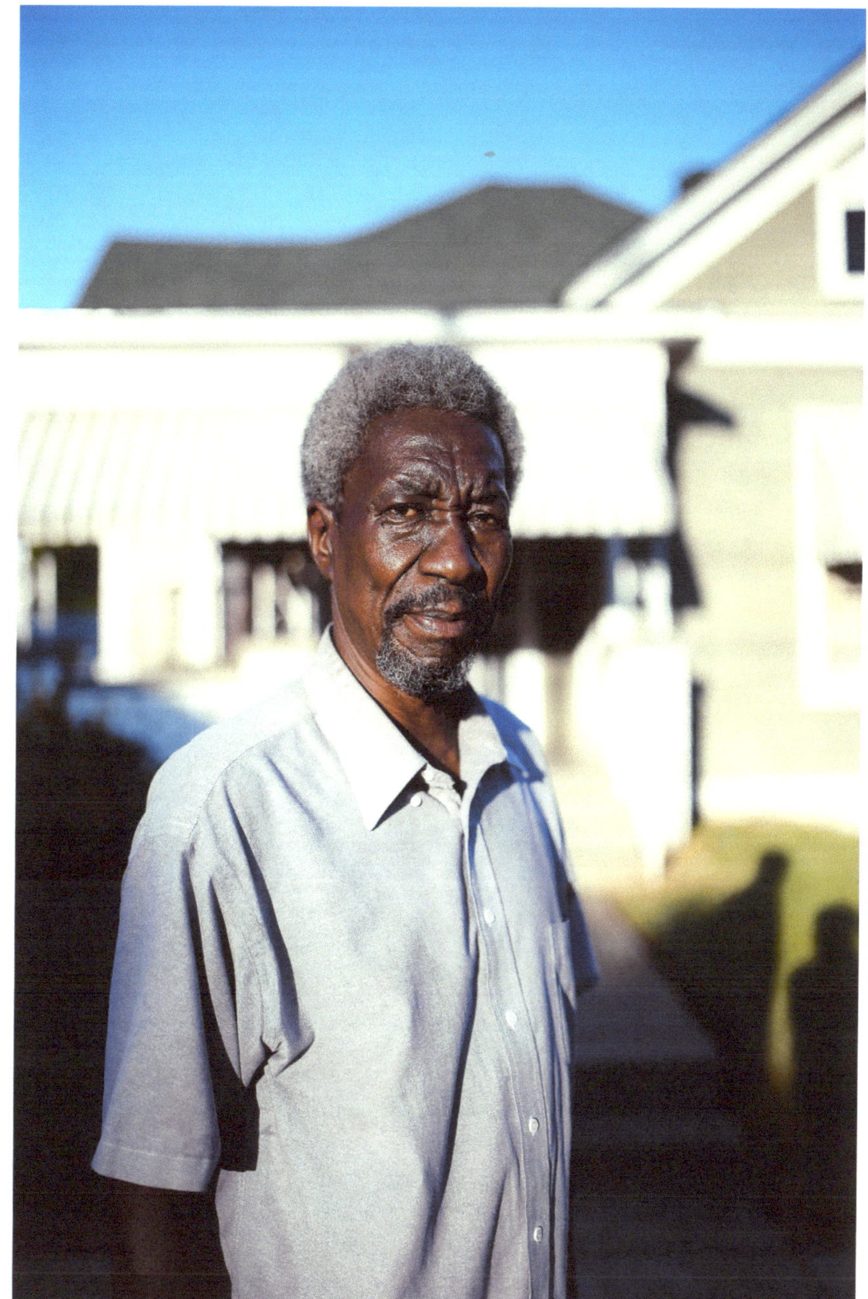

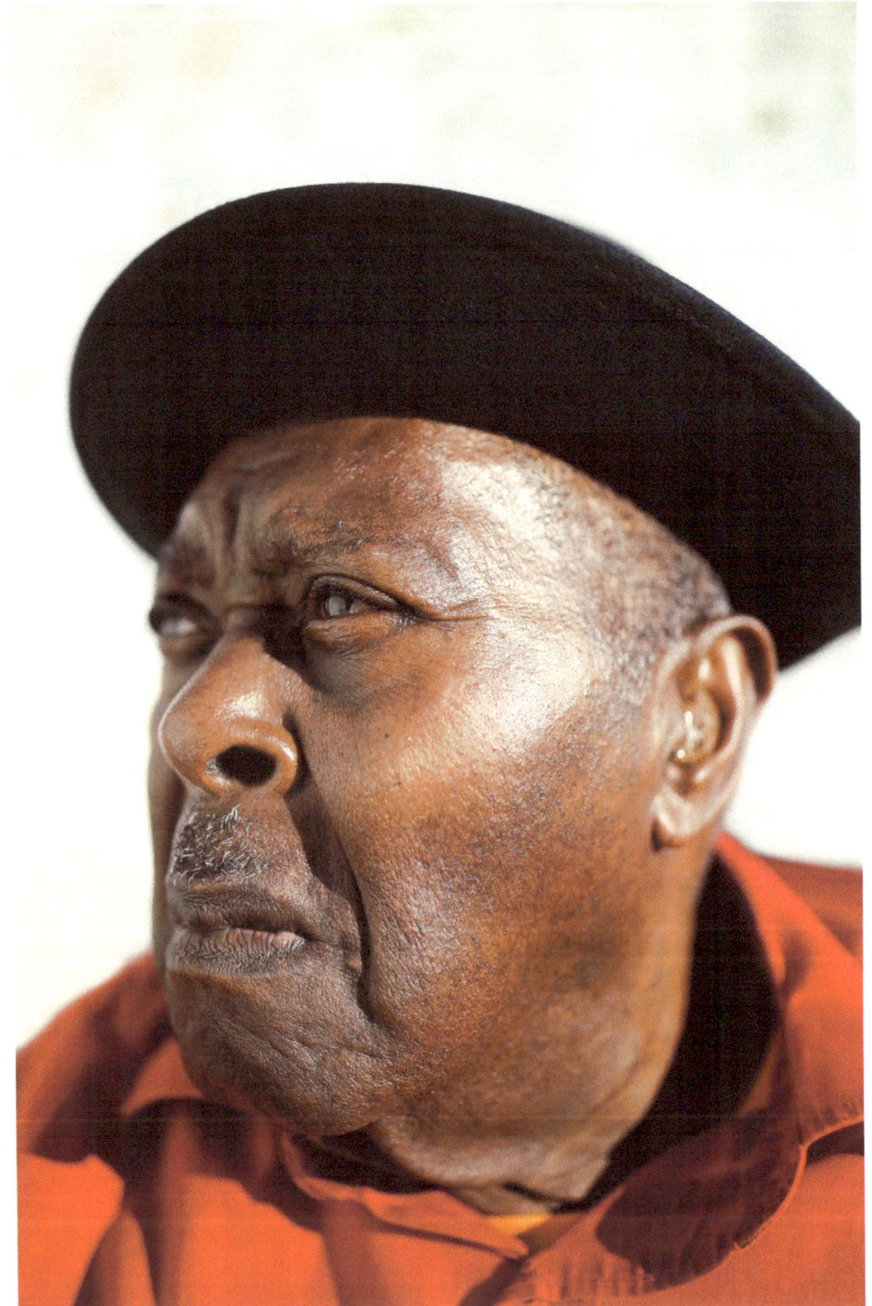

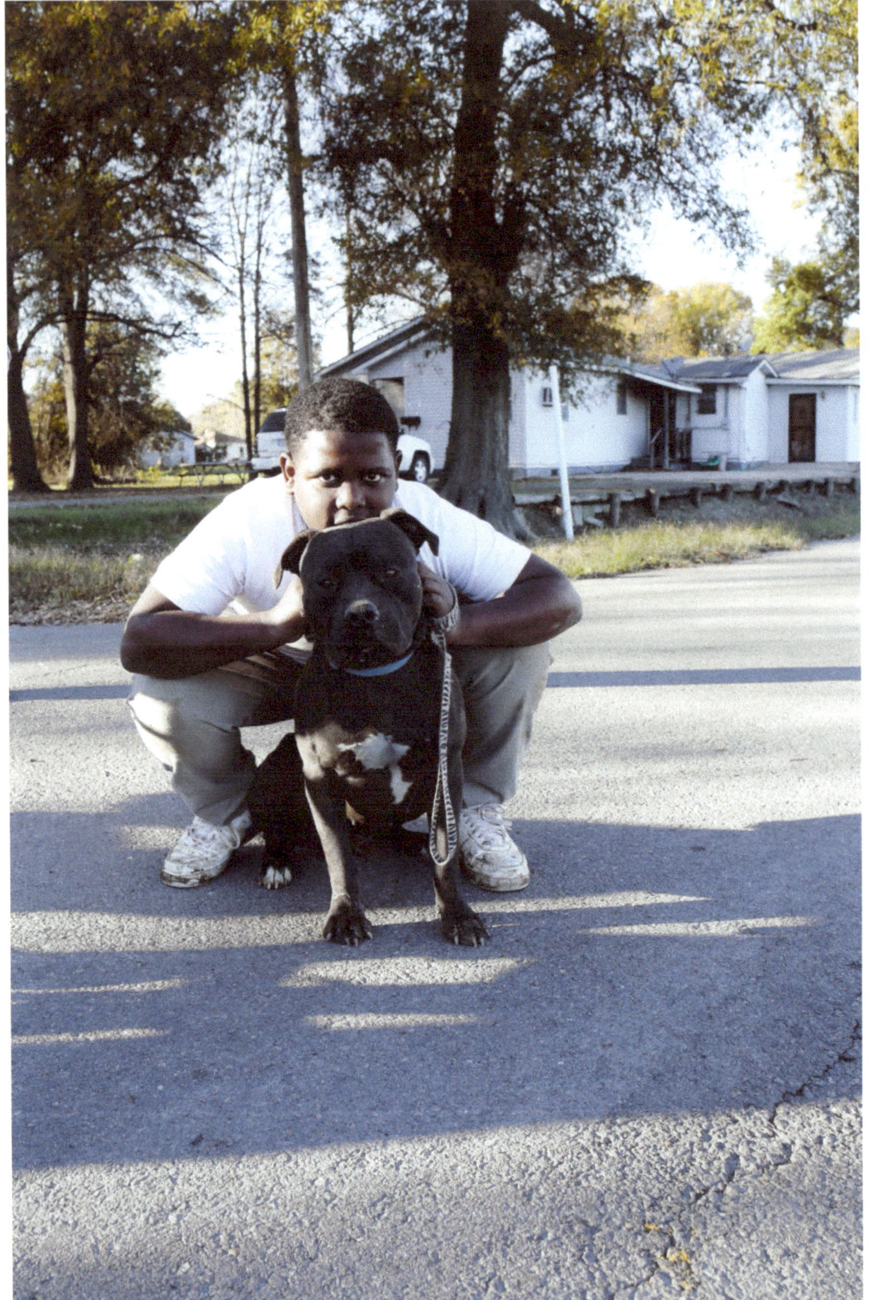

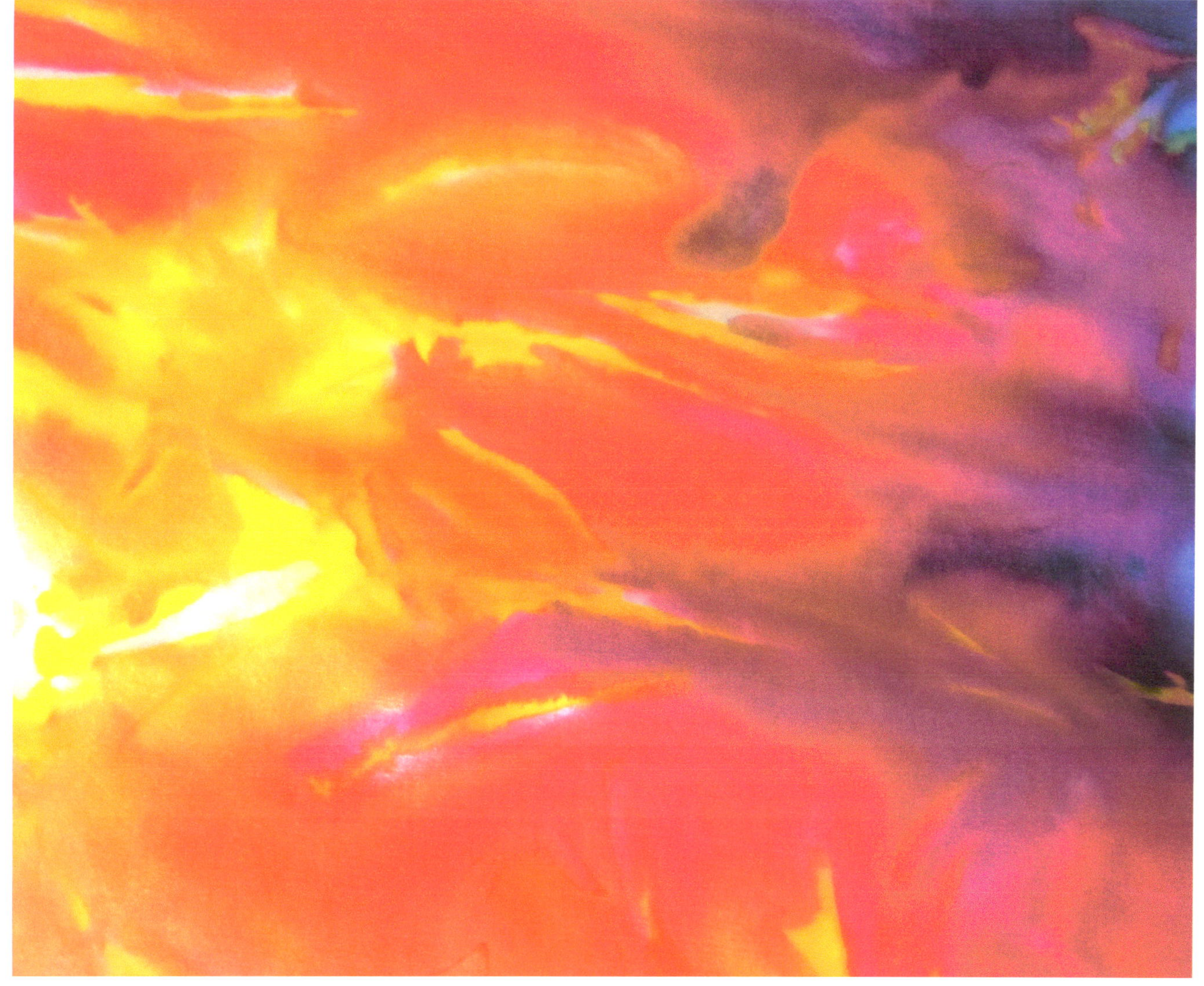

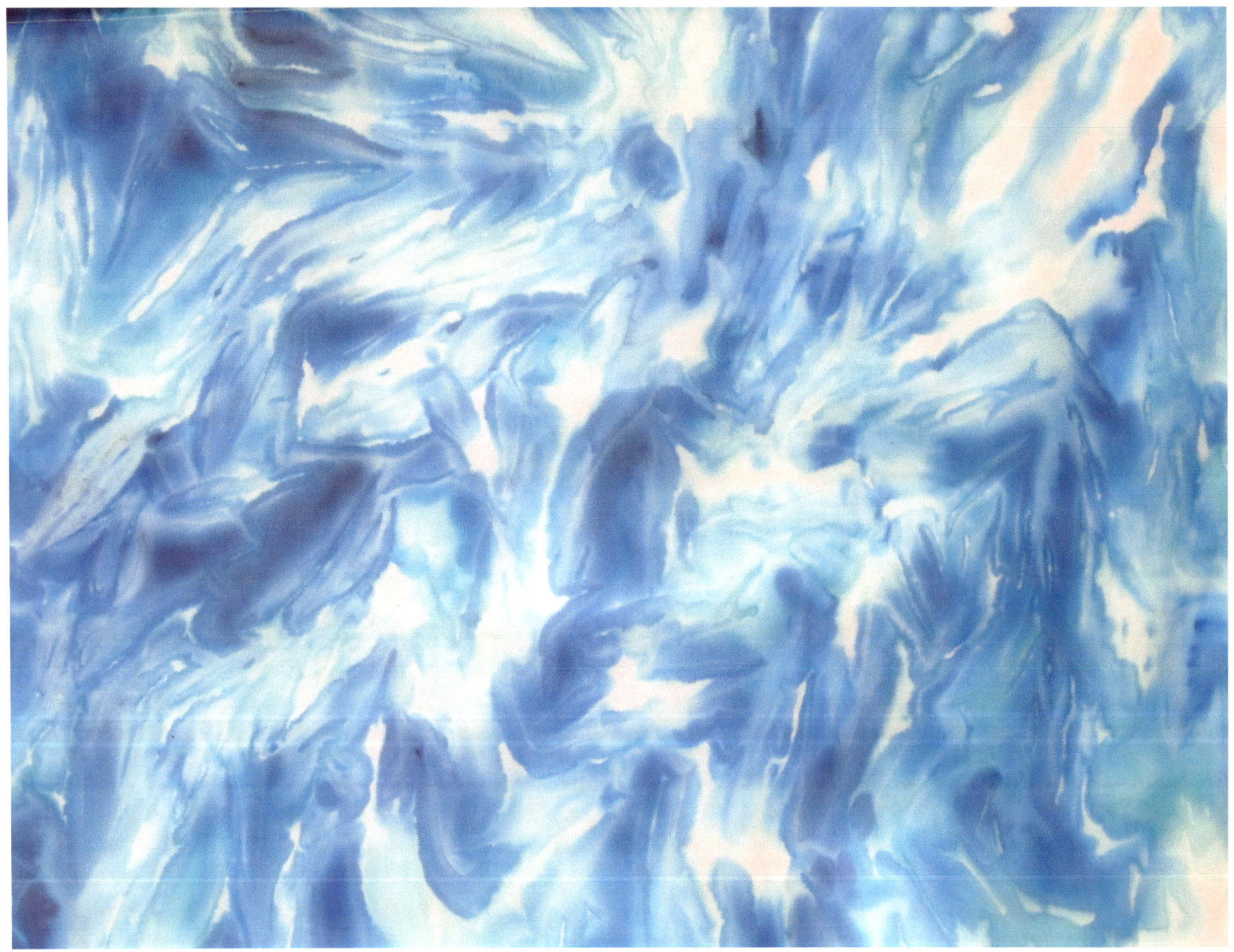

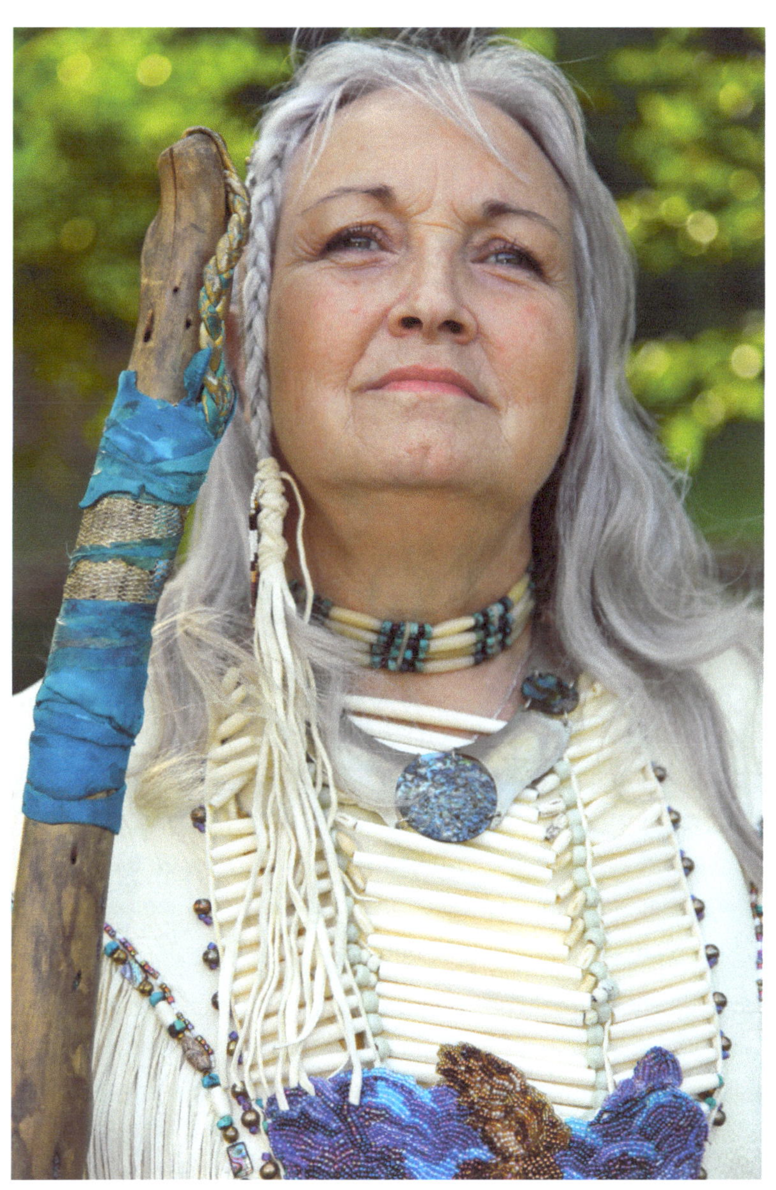

JOANNE MEEKS
Cherokee Roots

"Welcoming the New Day" — Traditional Cherokees would go to moving waters as the sun was rising - symbolically cleansing their spirit as the water washed their body. As they looked toward the sun, each new day was was filled with hope, endless possibilities, and vibrant life. *Hand-dyed silk.*

"Ripples In The River" — The river moves endlessly onward, swirling and flowing toward its destination, carrying life and hope within its depths. *Hand-dyed silk.*

"Ancient Blood" — Each individual is a mixture, a composite of the ancient bloods that flow through our being to make us who we are today, a multi-colored thread in the tapestry of life carrying a potential destiny that could impact the world in a positive way. *Photograph.*

BETHANY MAY
Poser

In 2017, I made a New Years resolution to attend 100 yoga classes. By the end of the year, I tallied 134 practices in a group setting. I had been a casual attendee of classes in the past and practiced sporadically at home before resolving to hit a certain number of public practices.

A few months ago, I attended my first yin yoga class. For 90 minutes, instead of flowing through planks, warriors, and down dogs, we sat on cushions in a candlelit room that smelled of bergamot and lavender oil and transitioned between postures we held for a long time, sometimes as long as ten minutes in one pose.

Yin yoga focuses on the connective tissues instead of the muscles, and though the scene is set for relaxation, opening the hips or shoulders deeply for a long time was uncomfortable. The experience, though, was pleasurable, not because I'm a masochist, but because I felt accomplished for sticking with it.

You aren't supposed to stay in the pose when it's painful, but you don't bail out of the pose when it gets hard or uncomfortable either. Instead, you breathe slower and deeper. It teaches you to do hard things.

I was diagnosed with Crohn's disease at 16 and have struggled with chronic pain ever since. I have surprised myself by doing hard, deeply uncomfortable things, by breathing, self-soothing, whispering to myself "you're okay, you're okay, you're okay." Over and over, faster and faster, trying to will it to be over quickly.

But in yin yoga, you pay money to enjoy and relish doing the hard thing and to do it slowly and intentionally. At the end of the practice, one of the assistants walked around the room to "show love" to our shoulders with a mini massage, readjusting the blades to lay flat against the floor and to get heavy on the ground while we lay in corpse pose.

The moments when you enjoy being in your body even in discomfort is new for me. But the commitment to showing up and breathing through poses a few times a week became an opportunity to marvel at my own body. The following essays are unapologetically and literally navel gazing, from the view of a downward dog or bridge, attempts to explore how sick bodies pose in the world of the well.

Though each essay explores a moment in my illness, I hope readers can identify with how wellness and illness alike shape our perspective of the world.

Mountain Pose

There's a pose in yoga that for the longest time I thought required just standing. It *looks* like standing. Your feet face forward on your mat (or on a sandy beach if you are one of the bendy, pretzel yoga girls that lives in an Instagram grid). Your legs are straight, hip-width apart, and your arms are usually hanging at your side with your palms facing forward.

After recovering from my first surgery, I joined a gym and started attending weekend yoga classes. When the instructor would call out "mountain pose" or *Tadasana*, her demonstration looked exactly like she was doing nothing but standing there in front of us. Sometimes she'd stand in mountain pose and swoop her arms up by her ears before swan diving her chest toward the floor and throwing her legs out behind her, landing in the top of a push-up.

I liked to reach up in mountain pose. At least with my arms toward the sky, I felt like I was doing something, with the potential energy of Da Vinci's Vitruvian Man moments before he starts making snow angels on the parchment or Moses holding his staff above his head while the Israelites crossed the bed of the Red Sea. With my hands reaching up, my arms might get tired, but I wasn't just standing there and waiting for the next pose.

Of course mountain pose, as I later learned, only *looks* like you're just standing there. "Push your feet into the Earth. Rotate the thighs inward, and lengthen the legs toward the floor. Don't lock the knees. Tuck the tailbone under. . . Bring the weight to the front of the heels, and then the breastbone points up. Try to touch the shoulder blades in the back, while pushing your shoulders down. No, not up by the ears . . . ," Tatiana, the petite Saturday morning instructor with a recognizable Russian accent, would call out a long list of instructions for getting alignment right, as if we hadn't been standing all our lives.

All that pushing, reaching, and rotating isn't obvious to someone watching the pose, but if you are doing it right, you *feel* the difference because mountain pose is work, albeit invisible work.

The day I felt the difference, I looked at myself in the gym mirror. I was expecting to see some change in my posture, however slight, that had made all the difference I was now able to feel, but my reflection was unchanged. Under my black yoga pants, the unshaved legs, the half-inch hole carved out of my left butt cheek, the starved muscles, and calcium-deprived bones were hidden. All the evidence that I was trying to be healthy, to be strong, to be there on the mountain, engaged, was invisible.

I should be good at mountain pose because I've had so much practice trying very hard to *not* look like I'm trying. Usually I'm trying to appear healthy or just not in pain. I don't usually look like a sick person, and so I'm always trying to keep up that appearance.

When I was 16, I was diagnosed with Crohn's disease, an incurable autoimmune disorder that affects the digestive tract—anywhere between the mouth and the anus, sometimes multiple places. A colonoscopy had revealed that the first part of my small intestine, the duodenum, and the last part, the ileum, were lined with little pink ulcers that looked like swollen shiny gummies. I kept the photos from my first colonoscopy and once showed them to my husband Adam when we first started dating. He was grossed out that I would keep them, but he stuck around anyway. And I still have the photo somewhere at my parents' house.

In between diseased sections, shingled with deformed cherry gummy bears, there were still large segments of healthy, smooth intestines.

I think it's funny and fascinating to have a little keepsake of when the disease was first growing in me, a baby picture of my illness. Since it's not obvious why there is a slow leak in my energy tank, I like a visual reminder than I'm not crazy and the sickness is real.

In online autoimmune circles, they talk about the spoon theory. It's a metaphor to explain the invisible work required to endure a chronic illness. The theory is credited to Christine Miserandino who wrote the essay "The Spoon Theory" in 2003. Miserandino lives with lupus, an autoimmune illness where the immune system attacks healthy tissue. In her metaphor, spoons are energy. Spoons are finite, and every task (taking a shower, getting dressed, going to the store, even sitting up) costs a certain number of spoons. Once her spoons are used up for the day, there is no energy left for anything else. There's nothing left in the tank, and fumes may be enough to pull the blankets higher around your shoulders, but they won't get you to the washing machine to clean the other dirty blankets and laundry piling up.

Of course, everyone's energy will eventually run out, even that of healthy people. But the spoons full of energy are invisible, and there's no way of knowing how much someone else starts with in the morning or how low they are running at a ny given point.

When you're sick, you have to use your already scarce spoons on enthusiasm because enthusiasm takes energy too. Deep breaths take energy. And before you know it, in the spoon economy, you've used them all just to ride out a wave of bubble gut, which is what I call the sensation of intergalactic forces blowing up the DeathStar of my stomach.

They say you are good at something when you can make it look easy, no matter how much effort actually goes into it. I sometimes wonder if I am good at being sick, if I am so good at it that it looks effortless.

I expended so much energy over the years hiding the gurgling and retching sounds of my body and bracing myself for the simultaneous coat of chill bumps and beads of sweat that follow. I hand over spoon after spoon, just to look like I'm standing there in mountain pose.

I think most people living with invisible illnesses are quietly standing on the mountain, muscles engaged, pushing, reaching, rotating all the time, making it look easy. We've certainly had plenty of practice.

The Italians have a word for the trying behind the scenes that makes whatever you are doing look easy. *Sprezzatura* is all the effort that goes into making something look effortless. It is the 83 photos you reject before posting one where you just so happen to look candid, carefree, and totally happy in the moment and not at all self-absorbed. It is the believable look of graciousness the skilled actor can summon when the camera pans to him at an award show where he was nominated for his talents. It is the nod and enthusiastic applause that communicates it is an honor just to be nominated and he is truly happy for the winner that isn't him. But mostly it's the fact that both of these reactions were practiced for hours in the mirror since the moment he heard he was nominated, maybe from the moment he knew he wanted to be an actor. *Sprezzatura* is the invisible work of being cool, charming, stylish, and enviable and destroying all evidence that it doesn't come easy.

Social media is the platform of *sprezzatura* because we're all trying to look like these candy-colored images, sun flares, and bubbly cocktails, to give the impression that the cottony clouds around the wing of the plane are the substance of our glamorous lives, rather than the tiniest of transitions between Wednesday night and Thursday morning at the office that will be much like every other Thursday at the office with a sack lunch, extra-strength Tylenol, and afternoon of spreadsheets. I am vain, so I want to look healthy and glamorous without trying, but I am also afraid that if it looks easy, I might be in pain someday and no one will believe me.

A few years ago, a model from the United Kingdom brought a lot of attention to Crohn's Disease, because she posted a photo of herself lying poolside in Bali. She had long, mermaid hair, big paparazzi-dodging sunglasses, tattoos on her arms and ribs, black bikini, and two colostomy bags on her thin, hourglass torso. Women's interest publications and health blogs and magazines published stories about her bravery for not hiding the poop pouches that saved her life after her bowel function failed. I clicked on every headline about her decision to share vacation pictures and the illness that led to almost a dozen surgeries, including the two stomas.

When I was younger, I'm sure I dreamed of holidaying on a beach somewhere like Townsend, but I never had any desire to wear a thong. Lately, I've been grieving the opportunity to wear a neoprene piece of floss between my butt cheeks while sunbathing. It's not that I can't, but now I have a scar on my butt from one of my surgeries that was necessary because of Crohn's complications. My days of playing volleyball in a skimpy Brazilian swimsuit like Gisele Bundchen were over before they even began.

I suppose I could still do it now if I wanted to. What once looked like a wound scraped out with an apple corer is now just a faded purple indention. I'd be called "brave" for showing what living with Crohn's could look like. There'd be headlines about how inspiring it is to see me living my life, not caring about the scar. I'd be just like the model Townsend, only not so thin or tattooed or tan or British. You'd know the truth, though. That I care too incredibly much. And I'd be holding in my stomach and tightening my thighs and pulling my shoulder blades together.

Posing on the mountain or the Brazilian beaches, I'd still be trying to look like I'm not trying.

Of course, the downside of making it look easy is that no one can tell you have volatile tectonic plates inside of you, nor when they're shifting. Plates break off and form new continents. You are sure the last one was an eight on the Richter Scale. You are shook, maybe a little pale, but your reflection is basically the same. To everyone else, you're just standing there.

Garland Pose

I had been married for three months in January of 2010 when we moved across the world from Little Rock, Arkansas, to Busan, South Korea, to teach English as a Second Language.

While we planned where to have our ceremony, we were also planning what we were going to do with ourselves after the wedding. We hated our recession-era jobs, but they offered health insurance. And pre-Affordable Healthcare Act, health insurance for someone with a pre-existing condition was not something you walked away from.

Every millennial knows this part of the story. I graduated in December 2008, and as I looked for writing jobs, every posting came with the same requirement: "3-5 years of experience." I had done a semester internship. I needed insurance, so I stayed at my retail management job that offered it. This was the logical decision. I was sick. And shrinking.

Years and years of bowel disease had turned the once-smooth muscles of my intestines into uneven cobblestone that couldn't digest anything but white rice and toast without pain and days of diarrhea. Inside the three-tiered blush wedding dress that had fit perfectly when I bought it, I was withering.

To get away from our crappy jobs and avoid losing insurance, we decided to move somewhere with jobs and healthcare. And also kimchi.

In preparing to move to Korea, I messaged someone from my hometown for advice. She had also moved to Asia to teach English. In addition to some tips about learning the language and the reputation of Korean schools, she told me to get ready to squat, because the schools where she had lived in China all had squatting toilets. That didn't turn out to be the case in Korea, but it did add to my anxiety about moving. Not only would I have to navigate a new city, new language, and new career, I would also need to revise my stance during my most basic functions: #1 and #2.

I think I only actually encountered a squatting toilet once the entire year of our contract in Korea.

It was in the subway station. Normally, I would cross my legs and hold my breath to avoid using public restrooms, but one night around 7:30 p.m. after a ten-hour day in the classroom, I couldn't hold it. My commute involved a five-minute walk to the subway station, then a 20-minute ride, and a couple more minutes of walking to my own toilet.

I was in a dress and heels, neither of which presented too much of an issue. The tights I was wearing, on the other hand, were a complication. I had to shimmy them around my ankles in order to squat low enough, but they bound my feet too closely together, restricting my movement. My experience squatting was cumbersome enough that for all future commutes, the entire year I was there, I planned ahead and stayed just dehydrated enough to not have to use the subway bathroom again.

Koreans, I decided, after my one and only attempt to squat over what looks like a urinal turned on its side and lowered in the floor, had better balance and more quad strength than I was capable of.

The makers of Squatty Potty™ have aimed to solve the problem that Western toilets create. There's an episode of Shark Tank in which a guy and his mom convince Mr. Wonderful how fabulous it is to poop in a squatting position and for the low, low price of $25, buy a plastic stool (they now come in the much classier bamboo and teak in sleek Scandinavian designs small enough for Brooklyn apartments) to fit around your Western toilet so you can lift your legs closer to your butt while you go. There were a lot of poop puns in the episode, which I mostly appreciated, like "our business is to help you do your business" and something about "a crapload of money." In the end, Lori gave the Squatty Potty™ business $500k for 10% share. I'm sure they're all very pleased with themselves for helping the Western world squat.

Squatty Potty™ is supposed to change your posture while defecating to more closely match that of our cavemen ancestors who didn't have indoor plumbing or even doors to demarcate indoor from outdoor anything. We're not living in the cave anymore, and that's supposed to be progress, so I don't know why we'd want to make our cave-dwelling ancestors some kind of pooping models.

It's probably something about evolution and the way we evolved to poop in squatting position and so because they squatted now we are programmed to poop that way until our bodies adapt to porcelain. But in two-thirds of the world, including Korean subway stations which are not wholly unlike caves, people still honor the shitty shitting tradition of our ancestors.

I definitely don't want to be disrespectful. We, who poop on a chair with a pipe attached, are the freaks, and the fact that someone has had to commercialize a plastic stool to correct our posture proves that. Even President Jimmy Carter got hemorrhoids, and proctologist Michael Frielich claims that there's a reason that in so many places in the world people still squat—it's because we were made to. At some point since 1592 when the throne-adjacent toilet was created, people experienced hemorrhoids and constipation and connected the maladies to sitting on the toilet.

The squatting posture, I think, is interesting even if I'd rather not balance with my tights around my feet. In my yoga class at the gym, almost all the instructors use English names for the poses instead of Sanskrit names except for *Shavasana*, which sounds better than corpse pose, I guess. I'm always intrigued by how *asanas*, or poses, get their names. Some, like triangle, are obvious descriptions of the shapes they make, but others like camel are as mysterious to me as constellations, cloud formations, and the inkblots in a Rorschach test. In an online forum where Wiki editors discuss the inclusion and arrangement of content in Wikipedia entries, I found a group of editors debating a theory about the etymology of one of the squatting poses in yoga.

In every class I've been in, the instructor has called out "Garland pose," and we line our feet up with the parallel edges of the mat before adjusting our toes outward and dropping our butts toward the ground, trying to keep our heels against the floor. Meanwhile, we press our hands into prayer at our heart and use our elbows to push our thighs and knees further out, opening up the hips. To me, garland is one of those names that doesn't describe the shape of the contorted body in this deep squat.

On the Wiki forum, one of the editors cited an online source that claimed the Sansrkit word *maalaasana* has been mistranslated to *malasana*. The former, *maalaa*, means excrement. As in "shitting pose." The latter, *mala*, means garland, necklace, rosary. The pose certainly resembles the position assumed when most of the world, including the Indian world, poops. However, the editors argued that the mistranslation is a fringe theory with a limited number of sources, and the far more accepted explanation is that the squatting posture looks like one is bowed down to accept a garland.

I tend to agree with the editors about distrusting information with so few sources but I like the idea of going to the gym and, between sweaty vinyasa flows, practicing the shitting pose with a dozen other yoga students in expensive Lululemon gear while a Selena Gomez song plays over the sound system. It would normally be something we'd be embarrassed about, but if we call it Garland pose, we'll pay $12 a class to squat in public with other gym-goers.

After moving to Korea, I had health insurance through my teaching job, but I hadn't achieved a healthy life. My anxiety about squatting to poop and pee was never realized more than once or twice, but I still couldn't digest much. For lunch, when my coworkers and I would walk down to the Orange Shop (what we called any mom-and-pop diner-type Korean restaurant—most of them had orange signs), by the beach near our school, I'd confound the waitress by just ordering "hana bap" or one small bowl of white rice. I'd douse it in soy sauce while my friends ordered steaming pots of "jjigae" stew or cheesy tonkatsu, dipping their chop sticks in a half dozen tiny dishes of kimchi, radish, and bean sprouts.

It was just easier to eat bland foods during the school day than to cross my fingers (and legs) that whatever I ate wouldn't send me running to the bathroom the teachers shared with the students, who were short and spry enough to crawl under the stalls or press their eyes to the cracks—both of which they absolutely did.

The private school, Wonderland Busan, where I taught all ages, kindergarten through teenagers, occupied two floors of a five-story building. During the morning, all of the kindergarteners were in classrooms on the first floor.

The kindergarteners left school at 2 p.m., before the older kids arrived for private lessons in English reading, writing, and speech presentation. Some of those classes were held on the fourth floor of the building where the second bathroom was. (The second and third floors housed some kind of kid's gym and a golf store.) The fourth floor bathroom was usually more private than the one on the first floor, but it was really cold in the winter. The window was either open or cracked, and toilet paper was scarce. Neither bathroom was a squatting toilet, but they weren't comfortable either.

With Crohn's you develop a kind of bathroom radar, immediately scoping out the most direct path to the cleanest, most private, best amenities. The upstairs bathroom of the school was okay in a pinch, but I really preferred using the facilities at the Popeye's across the street. The restaurant was never that crowded, so its second floor was rarely used. I'd go buy a biscuit on my break so I could use the bathroom upstairs without interruption from one of my students or coworkers. There was also a McDonald's at the top of the street, but it was always busy and a bit of a walk.

My sixth sense is to scan a new location for the best options as soon as I walk in the door so I don't have to waste time once I'm in pain. There're apps for that now—probably developed by someone with a similarly active bowel or just someone with a stake in the bathroom sector. Toilet paper peddler Charmin has one called SitOrSquat that uses your phone's GPS to locate nearby public restrooms. The flags on the bathroom map are crowd-sourced, so it's not a perfect system, as the app's success depends on its users finding and sharing information about the bathrooms they've used. The app designates a clean, desirable facility as a "sit" and a dirty or otherwise undesirable bathroom a "squat," which tells me that Charmin espouses similar feelings to squatting as I do.

A couple of years ago, I sent off for a wallet-sized card to present shopkeepers or others when a public restroom isn't available in order to persuade them to let you use their private facility. It says,

> "URGENT MEDICAL NOTICE. Please make your bathroom accessible. The person holding this card has a serious condition that makes it extremely difficult to wait to use a restroom. Crohn's disease and ulcerative colitis have painful effects so your help and understanding are crucial to the cardholder's wellbeing. Thank you."

I haven't used it yet because it's embarrassing enough to have to jet to a bathroom and most places, like Popeye's, have a public one available.

The fear of pooping in public toilets is called parcopresis, and I'm pretty sure I don't have it. With a real diagnosed fear, your body knows you're scared and can shut down your ability to urinate or defecate when others are just on the other side of the stall—shy bladder or shy bowel, they call it.

I think the anxiety for the general public is being the unlucky person to end up in a stall with a broken flusher or right after someone who has disregarded all signs that advise otherwise and flushed a tampon, clogging the toilet. Everyone will know you are a gross, disgusting human being with bodily functions.

If I do have toilet phobia, my body doesn't care and sure doesn't shut down the need or ability to go. I've been in public restrooms all over the world not because I have an eccentric bucket list to see every water closet on the planet; I've just got no choice.

Of course, parcopresis isn't paranoia. Sometimes, all your fears are realized, and you should have just stayed home rather than be forced to use the bathroom in an unfamiliar place like an unprivate, drafty stall at a school in Busan, South Korea, or a basement-level loo in Iceland during Valentine's dinner, which is the exact setting of my most embarrassing bathroom story.

After we finished our teaching contract in South Korea, we planned a week-long vacation in Iceland. To celebrate Valentine's Day, we booked a fancy dinner at Fiskfelagid in downtown Reykjavik.

The dinner was 5 courses prix fixe. Before each course, our waiter came over to our table, so dimly lit by a small candle, we could see the food in front of us and each other, but everything else was dark. The waiter explained where the venison was sourced and the lingonberries and the dairy from this or that sauce. Three courses in, an urgent, familiar pain unleashed rumbles through my abdomen, sent chill bumps up under my thermal underwear and down into my boots, and washed sounds around me like my head was suddenly dunked underwater.

I excused myself for the bathroom. There were two ladies' restrooms, and I used the one down the end of a long, dark hallway. After a few minutes, I felt better, washed my hands with the fancy soaps, checked myself in the mirror, and started for the door.

I turned the handle, and nothing happened. I tried the lock again, jiggling. Turning the little lever to the left and trying the handle and then to the right and trying the handle, I could not get it open. I stepped back and examined the lock. I knelt down and tried to figure out how it worked. Nothing. I knocked and knocked some more. I gave up and began again.

Eventually a staff member heard my knocking and started instructing me what to do, first in Icelandic and then in English, repeating all the things I had already tried. I was getting more and more frantic being stuck in a bathroom in an unfamiliar place with unfamiliar words being spoken to me.

Finally, he asked if I could open the window.

The restaurant was built into the side of a hill, and the bathroom was partially underground. The window was very high on the wall, but it was ground-level on the street outside.

I crawled up onto the sink, hoisting up my dress and stood all the way up on my tiptoes, and was just able to reach the window to get it open. Within a couple of minutes, the man who had been talking to me from the other side of the bathroom door was crouching down on the street outside and crawling in the window above me.

As embarrassing as all this was, I had not cried, but my face was hot. And though the window was letting in the Nordic winter air, my cheeks got hotter when he walked right over to the door and unlocked it in seconds.

Forty-five minutes after I had left the table in gastro distress, I returned to eat dessert.

It's a wonder that I don't have parcopresis after my bathrooms-around-the-globe experiences with a bowel disease. Instead of fear, I try to find it funny. Funny that I could engineer an "It's a small world" attraction that features the loo, john, water closet, baño, toilette, "little girls' room" of all the public restrooms in my travels.

And while I drop into a squat in yoga class and my thigh muscles burn, I sometimes think about the Wiki editors fighting over whether the pose is a bow to receive a garland or the much less reverent, but far more relevant to my life theory that the pose is named for someone pooping.

Pigeon Pose

After years of listening to my body so closely, questioning every degree on the thermometer, every ache, bump, tightness, and light-headed foggy feeling, one might think that I'd have more self-awareness about my own body.

But the story of my first surgery started long before I knew it, and I missed all the signs and months of symptoms leading up to it because you don't know what part of a story you are in while you're living it.

If I were to start in the middle of the action (the middle that I thought was the beginning), it would be a Friday morning in February 2015. I'd be on the floor of a St. Vincent clinic in the hallway to the bathroom. When I feel my peripheral vision darken, I crouch toward the floor. With the cool tiles beneath my fingers, I slide down onto my side, trying to get my head as low as possible so it will have nowhere to fall and nothing to hit when the growing darkness at the edge of my sightline finishes closing in.

Once on the floor, I realize I have spent all my energy getting down to avoid falling, but don't know how to get back up. So I call my husband, "Adam? . . . Adam? . . . Adam?" He hears me from where he is sitting on the other side of the wall in the lobby.

Adam finds me on the floor. He says, "What are you doing? You have to get up. You can't just lie on the floor."

I can barely get my brain to tell my mouth to say, "I can't get up. I'm too tired." I must look better than I feel because when he tells me to come sit down with him, I think *Can't he see my limbs are lead*?

Adam calls a nurse: "We need help."

Someone brings a wheelchair and gets me to the examination room. I thought I had the flu, but they tested me for strep and mono and flu—all negative. They tell me to go to the emergency room.

I had been feeling puny for several days leading up to the fainting episode at the clinic. There had been weeks before when I would come home from work and go directly to bed, no dinner, no shower, sometimes no changing my clothes. Adam had grown tired of my insisting it was just ordinary fatigue, and he was adamant we go to the doctor.

At the emergency room, masks were available at the front desk and were mandatory for anyone who had travelled recently to countries on the risk list. I don't remember what the pandemic was in 2015. Too early for ebola, too late for swine flu. It may have been Zika, but no one in the Little Rock St. Vincent Infirmary wore a mask.

I have trouble piecing that week together. I find myself listing things that happened, questioning the timeline, wondering if the situation was as dire as it seemed. My memory of the hospital is hazy for all the reasons hospital memories are usually cloudy for a patient: hunger, pain, morphine, boredom, and the heavy lethargy that I had carried in with me and that no one had diagnosed or offered to relieve.

Eventually, a big doctor with a thick Canadian accent told me I had an abscess in my pelvis. It was a pocket of fluid that had become infected and was making me sick.

I wasn't entirely blindsided by this information. I like to think that I am self-aware and know how to listen to my own body, and that part is true. I listen. I notice. I google to an unhealthy extent. Every slight discomfort I have ever felt has become a keyword in my most common search: low grade fever + crohns, sore groin + crohns, rash behind ear + crohns, fainting after standing up + crohns. I assume my autoimmune issues must be behind all of it. Googling makes me feel like a hypochondriac, but there's a nagging feeling that everything is related to the diagnosis I already have if I can just confirm it online. For months, I had been googling and obsessing over soreness and fatigue and intermittent fevers, but while I was noticing and listening to my body, I was also second-guessing it.

The seemingly innocent symptoms had been carving the pocket of pus and infection deeper for months, but the difference in intensity from one day to the next was barely detectable, like a frog in hot water, getting warmer and warmer. Until I was boiling with fever on the floor of that clinic.

To drain the abscess, a couple of orderlies wheeled my gurney downstairs. I may have been on too much pain medication to comprehend what was going to happen, but I don't think anyone ever told me. That probably happens in hospitals more than people realize. The doctors see you for less than five minutes a day, and the nurses all assume the doctors explained what's wrong and what will be done, what medicine you're given and how it's supposed to help. None of that happened to me though. Or if it did, the hunger, drugs, and boredom erased that memory, too.

The orderlies asked if I needed anything. I nodded no, and they left my bed alone in the hallway outside of a radiology room. I don't know how long I was parked there. Time expands and collapses on itself in these memories. When someone came out to get me, I was drifting in and out of sleep. They rolled me onto the table on my stomach. The anesthesiologist didn't put me back to sleep, but she gave me something that made me more agreeable and apathetic to whatever was coming.

I laid on my belly with my head resting on my hands, looking at the man to my left. He directed someone on my right, whom I couldn't see, to part my gown and pull my pants and underwear down around my thighs, but whatever drug was coming through my IV turned off my shame at being exposed. The man warned that I would feel pressure, but it wouldn't be pain.

I did feel pain, but I didn't have an eloquent way to communicate it then. I could only groan. Something very long and sharp had punctured my butt cheek and was now probing around in my pelvis somewhere. There was the pressure the man had told me about. I must have signed something but I don't remember giving consent to this because no one ever described what this was before I was face down, veins full of something that kept me just sentient enough to nod "Yes" and shake "No."

I whimpered over and over, trying to muster the most pathetic cries in order to communicate the pain. In that moment, the sounds I was making weren't just visceral responses to the sensation of my infection being pierced and probed. Without language, I was hoping there was some primal register of my bleating that could impart my wishes for him to stop.

When it was over, someone pulled my pants back up and rolled me onto my side before I was wheeled back up to my room. Waking up the next day, I found what looked like a plastic grenade hanging from the end of a tube the size of a pencil inserted into the skin of my butt from which the pressure and pain had stemmed the night before. Inside the grenade sloshed evidence of the infection. It looked like strawberry milk.

The weekend came and went. A nurse showed Adam and me how to twist off the plastic cap and drain the pink goo once a day. I lay on my side for a few more days in the hospital bed, afraid to roll over too far on my hip and disrupt the site where the plastic tube was draining the abscess. On Wednesday, I was discharged and told to come back in two weeks to monitor how I was healing and draining.

When we went home, I thought that was the end of the story, but the middle stretched on. I slept on my stomach or one side, and Adam helped me drain the bulb every night. I went back to work immediately, but Adam had to drive me so I could lie on my side in the car. For weeks at work I would lean on the arm of my desk chair so I didn't have to sit both cheeks down and push the plastic tube farther into the incision.

At the end of the day, my back and hips were sore from leaning, contorting, avoiding the left side for so many hours. I peeled off clothes when I came in the door to reveal indentions where the plastic tube and bulb had pressed too hard into the skin at my waistband, where I had been tucking it under my clothing.

The nurses in the hospital never mentioned changing the dressing around the surgery site. The skin was starting to break and get itchy. One of Adam's friend's wives, "St. Tara," who worked as a nurse at the Veterans' Hospital, came over to clean it and show us how to flush the line with saline.

I lay on the couch on my stomach, presenting my hind quarters like a red-butted baboon to a girl we had only been out with a few times. She gingerly dabbed it with alcohol wipes and pulled out a big box of rubber gloves, gauze, and other supplies to teach Adam how to care for it because I couldn't twist around that far to reach it myself. It was humiliating, but another one of those moments when I didn't have the self-awareness to know that my butt and body had stopped being a private, unblemished thing.

With the whole of my abcess story in the past, it is now clear that its real beginning was a year before I ended up on the floor of the clinic, when I was lying on the floor of my home office. My laptop sat just past the front of my yoga mat. One leg was stretched long and straight behind me, knee down like half of the splits that I once could do so effortlessly. In high school, I had spent many dance team practices warming up by sliding my legs out until my thighs touched the gym floor. My teammates and I would sing the theme song to *The Fresh Prince of Bel Air* as loudly as we could to distract us from the discomfort of waiting for our muscles to get hot and flexible enough for the choreography.

On my hot pink mat, while one leg was out behind me, the other was curled in front. I leaned forward over my keyboard and kept typing. At least once a week, I would assume this position and write for hours. I was a couple of chapters into my graduate thesis when I had to move my daily writing sessions from my desk to the floor. I had quit my job in an accounting office so I could spend the last semester of graduate school finishing my thesis while taking a full course load.

Self-care wasn't a buzzword yet, but I knew I was not being particularly kind to my body. I just wanted to get finished with my degree and out from under the deadlines and stress as soon as possible. I would drink coffee and energy drinks all night and stay up writing until 5 or 6 in the morning. All the anxiety about writing, graduating, getting hired or accepted into a PhD program was finding places to hide in my body. Usually, I could feel it in my groin, right where my legs plugged into my pelvis. To find relief, I started rolling out my yoga mat to stretch while working or procrastinating from working. I watched the whole last season of *House M.D.* on my mat one week between writing sessions. When Hugh Laurie would diagnose another mystery illness, I'd look up yoga poses to relieve hip and groin pain and try my best to imitate them.

Any position that stretched my hip flexors would do, but I found the most relief in the pigeon pose I had been doing while writing. Then I'd dig my knuckles into the crease where my legs met my pelvis, thinking my muscles were tight and I just needed to work them out like a masseuse kneading a knotty shoulder.

Pigeon pose has many variations. Some people puff their chest toward the sky like a bird and reach overhead for their back leg. Some relax their torso forward as I often did while trying to reach my laptop to keep working. If I really wanted to take care of my body, I might have stopped typing and gotten some sleep. Instead, I was a good pigeon. They are working birds who regularly carried information back and forth for humans during the 1800s. Carrier pigeons were integral to financial houses in England because their navigational skills and speed made them the fastest way to communicate business information. They're smart and self-aware, too. They are one of only six species to recognize themselves in a mirror—the only non-mammalian species to have this trait.

Of course, posing like a pigeon didn't make me aware of the trouble in my body. I thought it was hours of sitting at a desk that had made my hips stiff. I didn't know that the itch I was trying to scratch was the sack of inguinal lymph nodes in the groin that swell to alert the body when there is inflammation in the legs, feet, or pelvis.

These were the signs, messages, and warnings I was constantly ignoring, explaining away, that turned out to be important to the story of how infection got in and how I got used to flipping up my skirt, dropping my underwear, and mounting my butt on doctors' exam tables.

The day the doctors took the tube out, our driveway was covered in ice. Freezing rain and snow had closed my office, but I was determined not to miss my doctor's appointment. So Adam and I put on our parkas and snow boots and walked on the ice to get to the hospital.

Adam sat in the waiting room while I disrobed and climbed back up on a gurney. A doctor explained that we would look at how well the hole had drained and consider removing the tube to heal up. I was in the hallway outside the procedure room, separated from other waiting patients by a curtain.

The tube came out, and without having to tuck a plastic bulb of infected pink milk in my waistband, I kind of returned to normal life after we walked home through the snow and ice. Six weeks after they pulled the plug, I joined a gym for some real yoga lessons, not those instructed by my laptop, while I tried to treat mysterious lymph pain in the middle of the night. I was determined to know my body better than I had before, to listen more closely when I had the urge to roll out a yoga mat in the middle of the night, learn to recognize the signs of danger, and to take seriously the information the pigeons carry.

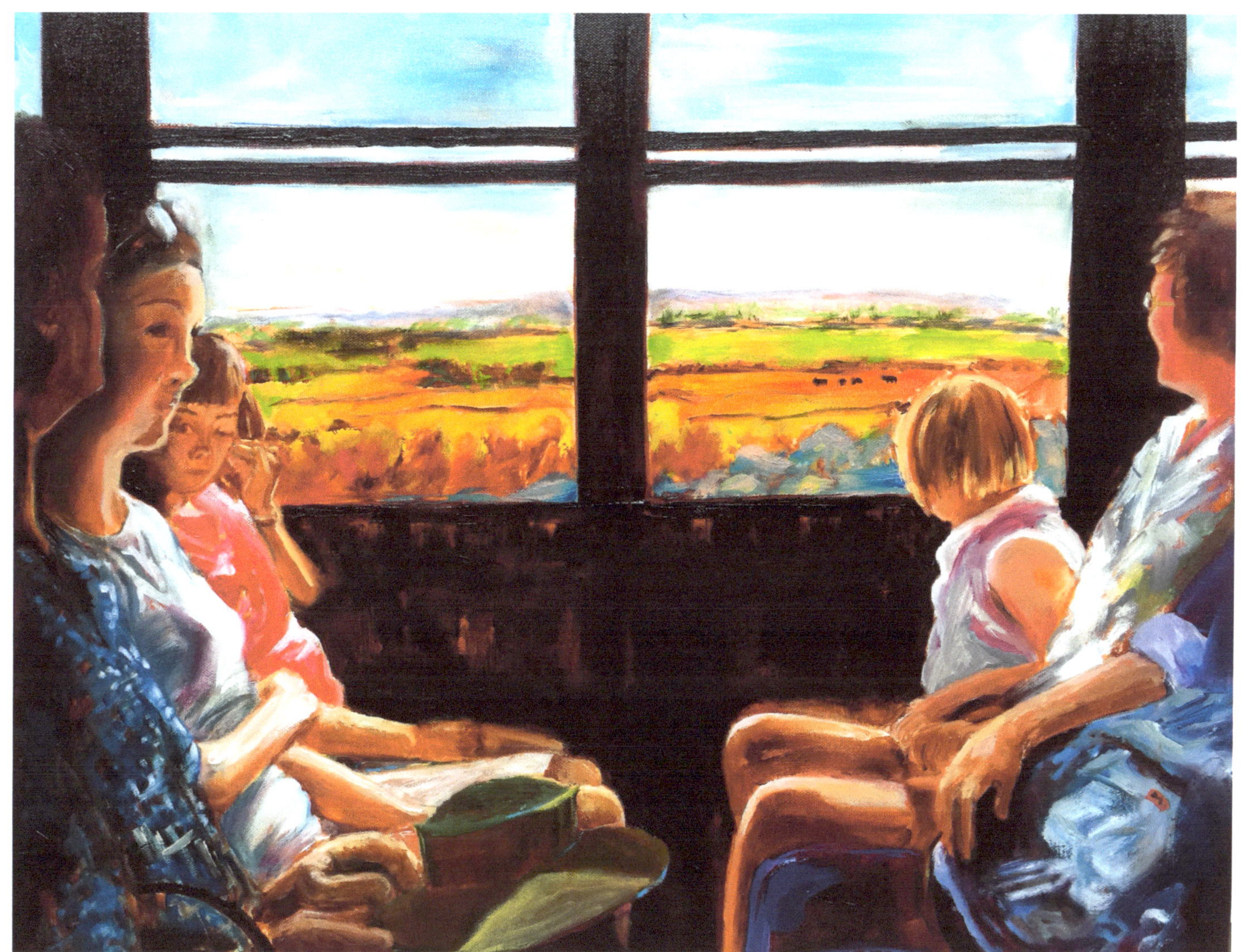

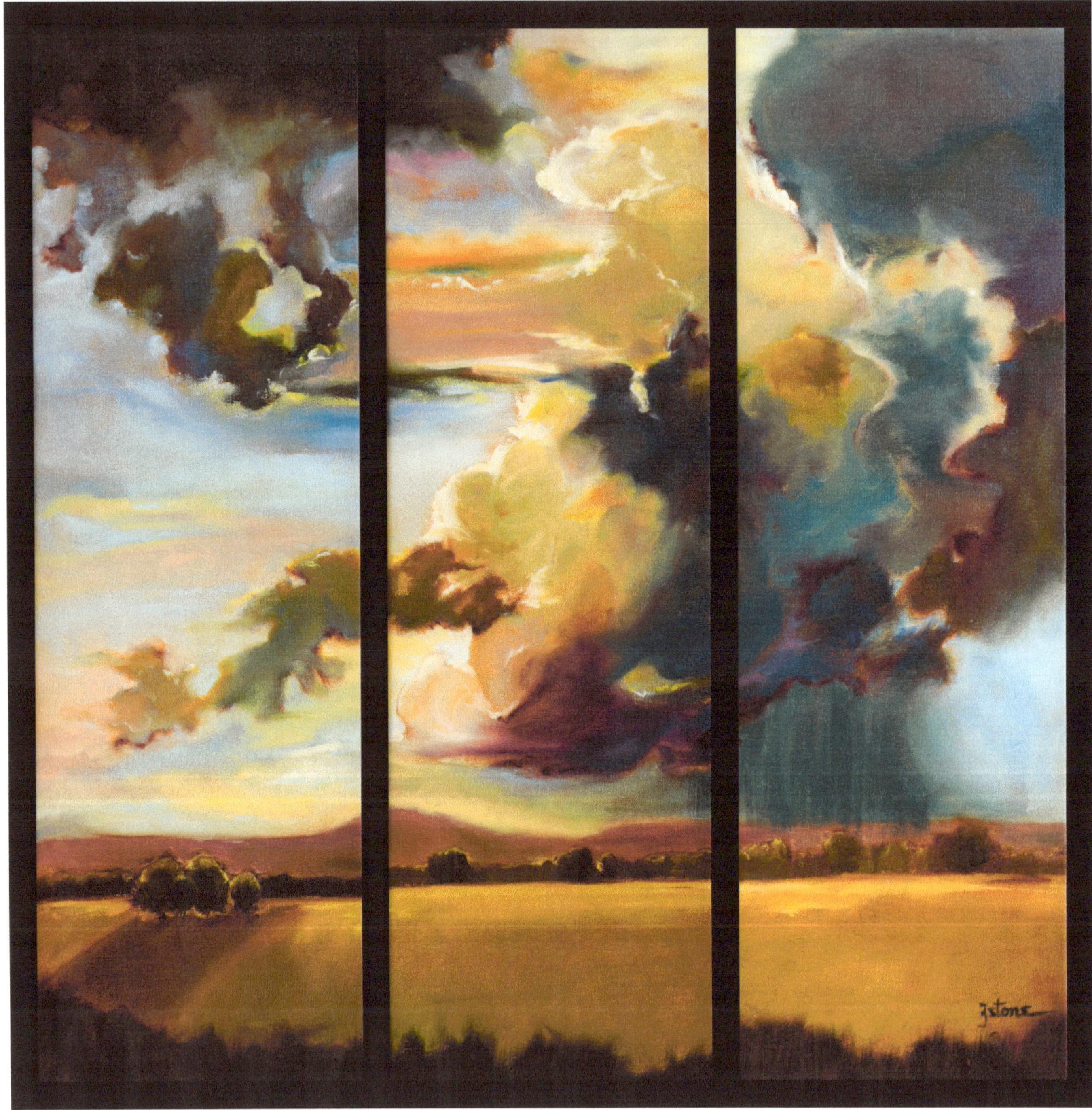

JEANNIE FOWLER RODRIGUEZ STONE

These oil paintings focus on Arkansas places. Each work carries a narrative about our resilience as a people, but also about our sacred connection to the land and—whether we want to admit it or not—to each other.

I am an Arkansan with Puerto Rican roots. When my family moved to the state in 1964, I was three-and-a-half. Spanish was my birth language but my father, an Arkansas native, forbade my mother to continue to speak to me in Spanish. That was a hard time in the South to be an "other," and my mother paid a price. In the end, however, her ability to speak four languages and the fact that she was Latina and a recent college graduate landed her a job with the Clinton Gubernatorial Staff. She later served in D.C.

As a mother of a deaf transgender son, I have also experienced a shunning in the rural community where we have lived for twenty-four years. Even at my age, I have returned to college and am a second-year student in the Interdisciplinary PhD Leadership program. My focus is on community-building through the arts. I have dedicated the rest of my life to using my art to build bridges, particularly in the rural parts of the state, and to re-introducing the lost art of neighborliness that front porches once accomplished.

CONTRIBUTORS

Chelsey Becker graduated summa cum laude from the University of the Ozarks in Clarksville, Arkansas, where she received degrees in art and business administration. A 2013 summer program grant gave her the opportunity to attend Frogman's Print Workshop to learn Japanese printmaking technique. In 2014, a second grant enabled her to participate in Southern Graphics Council International (SGCI's) annual conference, at which she was a presenter, and later to attend Sotheby's Institute of Art where she took a course covering the fundamentals of the gallery business. In summer 2017, Chelsey took the Advanced Painting Intensive course at Columbia University.

Megan Blankenship lives in the Ozark Mountains. She is the recipient of the 2018 Margery Davis Boyden Wilderness Writing Residency and a 2016 Arkansas Arts Council Individual Artist Fellowship. Her work was awarded the 2015 Meridian Editors' Prize in Poetry and has appeared in *Blackbird*, *The Missouri Review*, and *storySouth*.

Originally from Black Oak, Arkansas, **Justin Booth** splits his time between Little Rock and Austin, Texas. He is a writer of outlaw poetry, and the curator and host of Dive Bar Poets, a monthly reading series with residency at The White Water Tavern. Formerly a homeless I.V. drug addict, his work reflects the exciting hardscrabble life he has lived. He has multiple books of poetry: *Trailer Park Troubadour* (2013), *The Singer, The Lesbian, & The One with the Feet* (2015), *A Quarter, a Dime, and Two Copper Pennies* (2015), *Outlaw Blue* (2016), *Lucky Strikes, Grave Dirt, and 1/3 of the Stars* (2016), and *The Stripper's Daughter* (2017).

Wendy Taylor Carlisle lives with her husband on a hillside in the Arkansas Ozarks. She has an MA in History from the University of Arkansas, Fayetteville and an MFA from Vermont College of Fine Arts and is the author of *Reading Berryman to the Dog* and *Discount Fireworks* (2000, 2008 Jacaranda Books.) and five chapbooks, most recently *They Went Down to the Beach to Play* (Locofo Chaps, 2017). Her book, *The Mercy of Traffic*, is forthcoming in 2019. Her work is widely available on line and has been anthologized. For more information, check her website at www.wendytaylorcarlisle.com.

Wendy says: "I have lived in Arkansas off and on since 1973 (always calling it home since then) and since 2010 full time. No matter where I was exiled, I kept my Arkansas driver's license and I was always trying to get back home."

Meikel S. Church is a North Little Rock, Arkansas-based collage/mixed-media artist who challenges concepts of perception through his artwork. Meikel started creating collage in 2013 and quickly became addicted to the absurdity of taking found images, mostly from old books and magazines, and reimagining the meaning and context of the original intent. Meikel is drawn to old, stained, worn, rusted, and torn images. These imperfect images are really about life and living. The creative possibilities are endless. The main themes of Meikel's work are hellos and goodbyes in all of their glorious incarnations.

Todd Herman (Neglected Histories of Arkansas Contest art/photography judge) served as Executive Director of the Arkansas Arts Center from 2011–2018 before joining The Mint Museum in Charlotte, North Carolina, as it›s President and CEO. He was previously chief curator for six years at South Carolina's Columbia Museum of Art and worked for seven years at the Cleveland Museum of Art. Herman has held two Samuel H. Kress Fellowships and has taught art history at universities in Italy, South Carolina, Virginia, and the Midwest. Focuses during his tenure at the Arkansas Arts Center include an emphasis on increased access to the arts for everyone and expansion of educational outreach.

H.K. Hummel (Neglected Histories of Arkansas Contest manuscript judge) is an assistant professor of creative writing at the University of Arkansas at Little Rock and founding editor of Blood Orange Review. She is the author of Boytreebird and Handmade Boats, and co-author of Short-form Creative Writing: A Writer's Guide and Anthology (Bloomsbury, 2018). Her poems have recently appeared in The Hudson Review, Meridian, Booth, and Iron Horse Review. Visit her website at www.hkhummel.com.

Saira Khan is a writer, cartoonist, and photographer. She is currently working on a young adult novel, managing in retail sales, and giving her Doberman her best life.

Born in Newport Arkansas and raised in the rice fields of rural Jackson county, **Ed Madden** is a professor of English and director of the Women's and Gender Studies Program at the University of South Carolina. He is the author of four books of poetry, most recently *Ark* (Sibling Rivalry, 2016). His poems have appeared in *Crazyhorse*, *Prairie Schooner*, and other journals, as well as in *Best New Poets* 2007 and *Hard Lines: Rough South Poetry*. In 2015, he was named the poet laureate for the City of Columbia, South Carolina.

Bethany May is the managing editor of the award-winning trade magazine *Arkansas Trucking Report* and spends her days telling the stories of men and women who deliver freight across the U.S. You can find her non-autobiographical writing at www.arkansastrucking.com. Bethany studied writing and editing at the University of Arkansas at Little Rock and has been obsessed with storytelling since her first failed writing assignment, penning Mary Kate and Ashley fanfiction in third grade. When she's not writing, you can find her on a yoga mat practicing headstands or studying a map looking for the next great adventure with her husband, Adam, and researching where the best bathrooms are in every city they visit.

Brandon Markin is a photographer and writer, based in North Little Rock, Arkansas. He is primarily focused on telling stories that illuminate the human experience, through documentary photography, journalism, and portraiture. Brandon has been featured in a variety of publications, and his exhibitions include: *We Dissent: An Exhibition of Protest Photography, Visual Anthropology: Welcome to my Neighborhood, Instant Magic,* and *100 Years of Light in the Pines.* He is also a husband, father of two, and always up for a journey. Visit him at brandonmarkin.com.

Joanne Meeks was born in Northeast Arkansas in 1949 and lived in Jonesboro or Hot Springs for nearly fifty years. She traveled the southeastern states for the next ten, moving back to Arkansas in 2010. Proud of her mixed Cherokee heritage, Joanne's art and teachings carry that indigenous influence to release life and hope. She believes that art speaks, often bypassing intellectual misconceptions by communicating straight to the heart, especially on cultural and collective consciousness issues. Joanne releases truth and hope as a conference speaker, using storytelling and art to convey her message.

Maxine Payne is a photographic artist living and working in the foothills of the Arkansas Ozarks, where she was raised by her grandparents. Exploring life within communities both familiar and strange, she documents the richness of vernacular cultures in all their peculiar glory. She is a professor of art at Hendrix College in Conway and was formerly chair of the art department. Visit her at maxinepayne.com.

Maxine says, "Mean mommas and daddies build character, but don't ever be one. Sometimes character is overrated."

Laura Raborn's paintings have been exhibited throughout Arkansas and are in numerous collections including recent acquisitions by the CARTI Collection, the Arkansas Children's Hospital, and the Bill and Hillary Clinton private collection. Her work has earned numerous awards such as the Wilma and Jack Diner Purchase Award at the University of Arkansas at Little Rock. She has a thriving portrait commission business, one of which was presented to the former Governor of Arkansas, Mike Beebe.

After receiving a B.A. from Rollins College, Laura worked in marketing for six years and took evening classes at the Arkansas Arts Center, where she is delighted to now teach workshops. She recently completed her Masters in Art with a focus on Painting, during which she worked as a Graduate Assistant for the esteemed Dr. Floyd Martin at UA Little Rock. Her studio is open for appointments and her paintings can be viewed at www.laura-raborn.wordpress.com or by visiting Cantrell Gallery in Little Rock. Justus Fine Art in Hot Springs and Princess Street Gallery on Harbour Island in the Bahamas.

Jeannie Fowler Rodriguez Stone was born on a Navy base in Maryland and lived as a young child in Puerto Rico, her mother's homeland. She grew up in North Little Rock and has lived Arkansas since 1964. She graduated from Mount St. Mary Academy, attended Lyon College, University of Arkansas at Little Rock, and Arkansas Tech University. She earned a bachelor's degree in fine art, a master's in liberal arts, and is working toward her Ph.D. in interdisciplinary leadership from University of Central Arkansas. She is married to a small-town physician, is a mother to four sons, and is an artist, poet, and freelance writer for a regional magazine. She founded and directs a nonprofit agency that works to bring cultures together in rural spaces—Traveling Arts Fiesta. Her desire is to work with rural communities to create capabilities so that more Arkansans are able to reach self-actualization and enjoy a higher level of well-being.

Matt White is the co-proprietor of one of Little Rock's oldest beer joints and music venues, the White Water Tavern. He is a photographer of people and places across the American South.

Erin Wood (Editor) owns and runs Et Alia Press in Little Rock, and is a freelance writer and editor for a range of business and creative writing clients. She is editor of and a contributor to *Scars: An Anthology* (Et Alia, 2015), which assembles 40 works on scars of the body. Her *Women Makers of Arkansas* project, featuring 50+ women creatives, is forthcoming from Et Alia spring 2019. Her writing has appeared in *Catapult*, *The Rumpus*, *Ms. Magazine*'s Blog, *Psychology Today*, *Entropy*, *The Woven Tale Press*, and elsewhere, and has been a notable in *The Best American Essays*. Visit her at woodwritingandediting.com and etaliapress.com.

www.ingramcontent.com/pod-product-compliance
Lightning Source LLC
LaVergne TN
LVHW072329100826
845147LV00005B/663

* 9 7 8 1 9 4 4 5 2 8 9 6 6 *